R. James Woolsey

6-20-2009

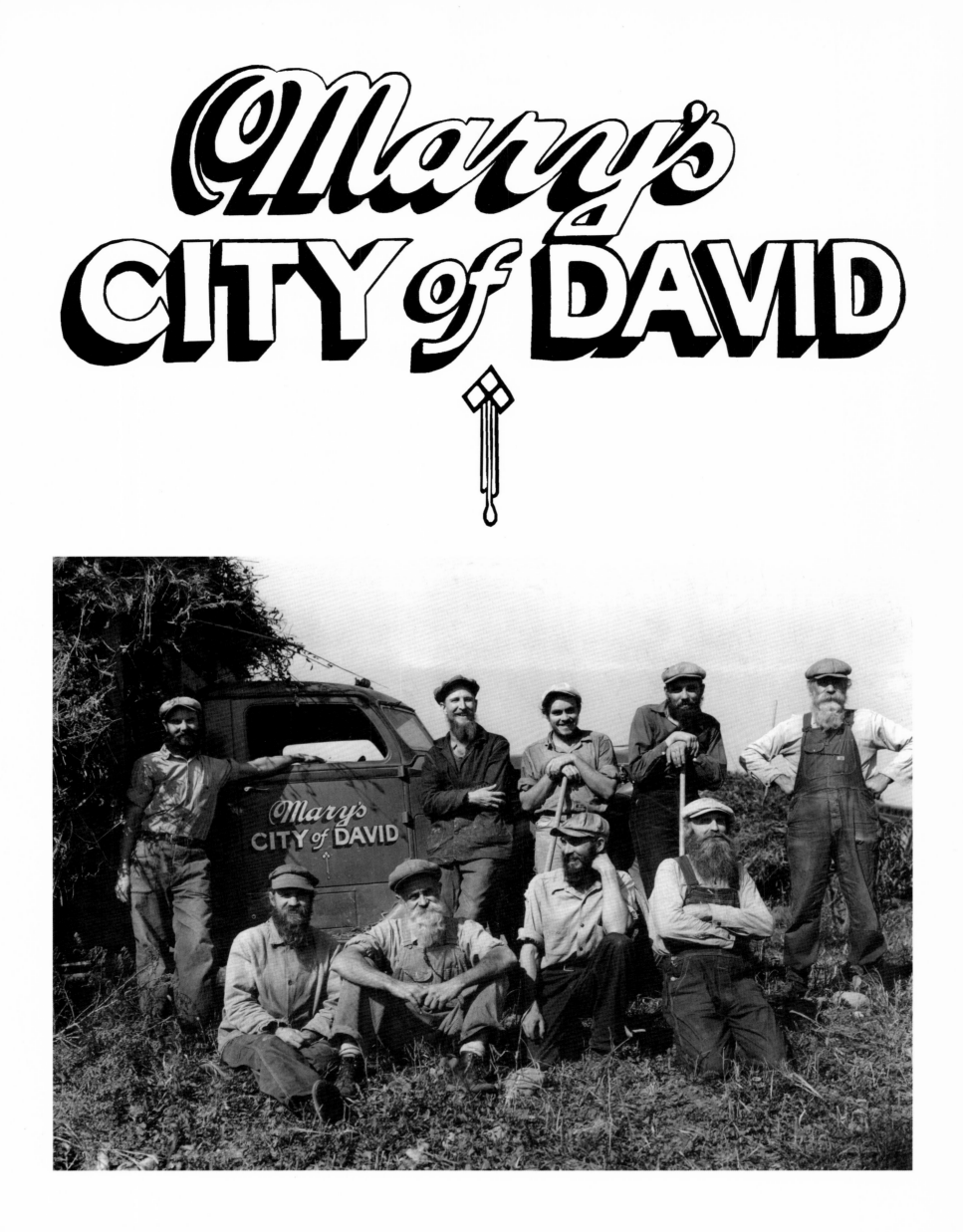

Copyright (c) 1996 R. James Taylor
Published by Mary's City of David
Benton Harbor, Michigan
All rights reserved.
ISBN 0–9653055–0–3

Mary's City of David

Table of Contents

Picture from September, 1940, taken by Fred Jolly of the Caterpillar Tractor Co., Peoria, Illinois. Lettering on the farm truck door was done by lettering artist commonly called "High Pockets," which lettering constitutes the title of this volume: *Mary's City of David*.

Dedication

This brief volume is dedicated to the faith, courage, determination, and long hours of unpretentious sweat that has stood, and still stands, behind the 396 signatures in the Roll Book of Mary's City of David. Common folks from all walks of life, because of faith and a fundamental desire to live according to it, created a city within itself, provided the surrounding communities with a plus in economic growth during the Great Depression, and gave Berrien County one of the most interesting and colourful chapters in its history.

Two citations of merit I will justly include in this dedication. The first being to Sister Eunice Bond, who I had known from early childhood, and more particularly in the last 18 years of her life; she being the finest example of Christian-Israel that I have ever known, in daily, faithful sincerity. One of the truly beautiful people, among the many in the fellowship, and commonwealth of Israel. Brother Francis Thorpe, whose diary and record keeping, from 1929 through 1957, is what has made the factual dates, names and events (as they were recorded) written in this volume, possible.

Preface

In a conversation with Mr. Clare Adkin, upon the completion of his work, *Brother Benjamin*, 1990, he stated to me that after his years of collecting information, materials, pictures and interviews, his greatest discovery in the entire history was Mary Purnell.

This is a story that finally needs telling to help relieve an uncertain and incomplete record, as well as to quiet the circulation of misinformation. Simply in this brief presentation of fact, to let a story be heard from the lips of those what were present in their daily lives of joys and sorrows, of success and failures, who know it best; because they were there.

This volume is the voice of their words, as was told to me over the past 26 years. These are the pictures of their labours in faith, daily in fellowship with the most outstanding and colourful lady in Berrien County's history.

"As the body without the spirit is dead, so faith without works is dead also." The Apostle James, in the second chapter of his General Epistle, shows the proving of faith is through works, in fact, "by works was faith made perfect."

Both the truth and immediacy of this volume are in view of the inspiration and power of a sincere and dedicated faith in God, which, through the many hands of long hours built the visible work of their faith, the City of David.

1 April, 1930 would be the third time Mary Purnell would leave a home setting by choice of conviction, with the breaking of Spring, stepping out into the unknown, without securities. At 68, having survived both of her children and her husband, she chose to leave behind the homes and properties that she, and the 217 with her, had worked for 25 years to build. The Ensign of faith was risen in the face of economic collapse, worldwide, with hardships in sacrifices as a daily menu. Now would be seen the true magnificence of faith, in its workings through trials of adversity, that surely are most necessary to bring it to light. The City of David, in its building of the 1930's, is the signature of this fellowship; and in all of the Seven Churches, over the history of now 200 years, is there not to be found a more clearly visible example of faith proven by works. A city built on a hill that cannot be hid; a working, and therefore living, faith, unto this day. As "by works was faith made perfect," so it is through the Living Faith (the body with the Spirit) will "patience have her perfect work." James 1:4.

Sister Mary Purnell

The Century of Seven Angels

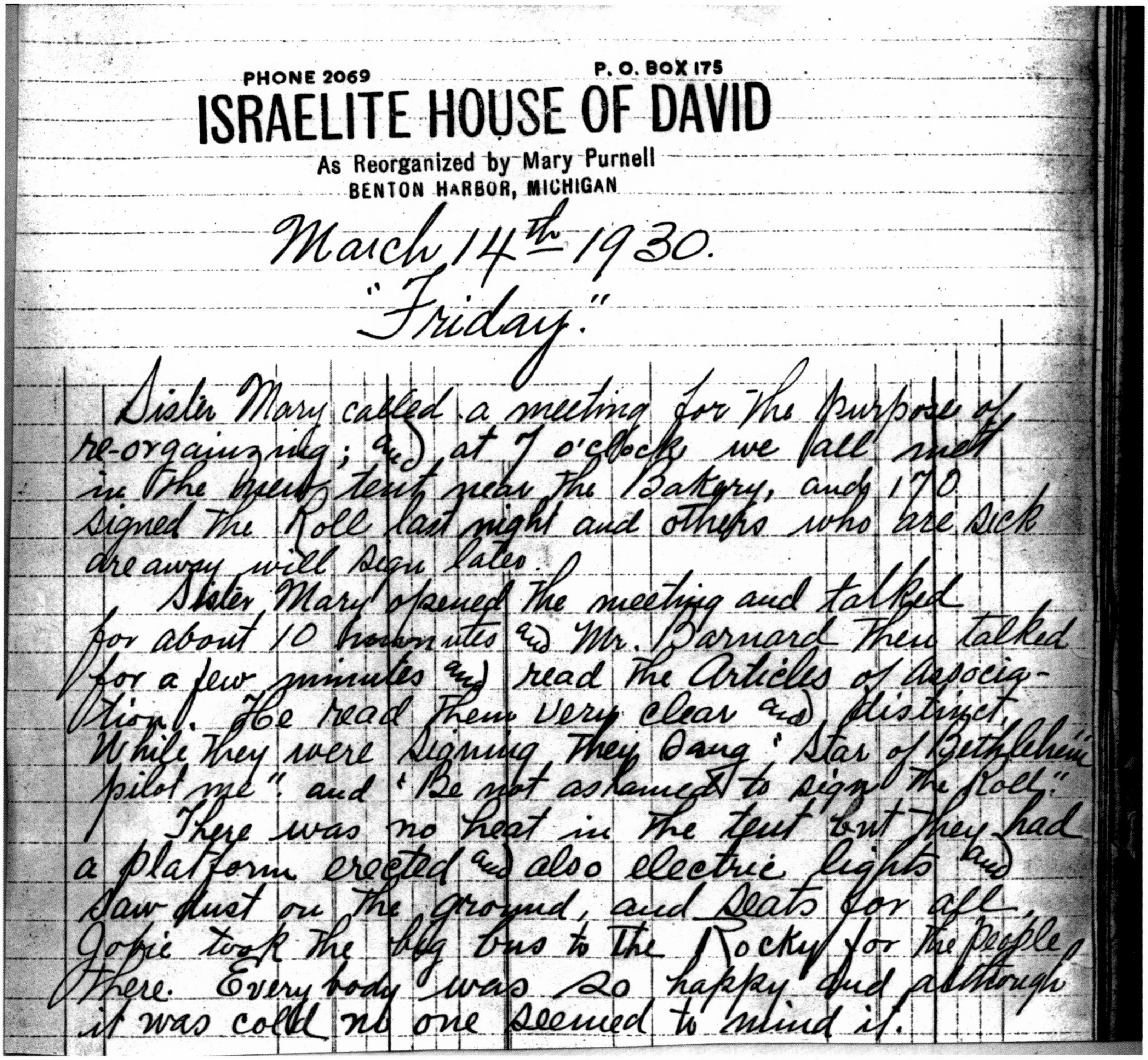

PHONE 2069   P. O. BOX 175

ISRAELITE HOUSE OF DAVID
As Reorganized by Mary Purnell
BENTON HARBOR, MICHIGAN

March 14th 1930.

"Friday."

Sister Mary called a meeting for the purpose of re-organizing; and at 7 o'clock we all met in the new tent near the Bakery, and 170 signed the Roll last night and others who are sick are away will sign later.

Sister Mary opened the meeting and talked for about 10 minutes and Mr. Barnard then talked for a few minutes and read the Articles of Association. He read them very clear and distinct. While they were Signing they Sang "Star of Bethlehem pilot me" and "Be not ashamed to sign the Roll."

There was no heat in the tent but they had a platform erected and also electric lights and Saw dust on the ground, and Seats for all. Josie took the big bus to the Rocky for the people there. Everybody was So happy and although it was cold no one Seemed to mind it.

And so it was 14 March 1930, in a large and new tent upon a clearing along Eastman Avenue, the Roll of membership was signed by 170 of the 217, and the re-organization had its birth. The beginning hours of the Israelite House of David as re-organized by Mary Purnell were meager, humbling and powerful in the midst of worldwide Depression, and the sore defeat of losing their beautiful homes that many among those 217 had built and lived in for over a quarter century.

From Francis Thorpe's diary for 1929-1930

Mary (Stallard) Purnell, photographed around 1875; her father, James Stallard would take his family of 8, shortly after Mary's birth in 1862, out of war-torn Virginia into neutral Kentucky in 1863.

With four farms, an unfinished hotel building in downtown Benton Harbor, two parcels of land on Eastman and Britain Avenues, and with little cash on hand, Mary Purnell began once again to build a home for her brothers and sisters of the Israelite faith, almost 27 years to the day that she and her husband, Benjamin Purnell, in a party of seven, arrived in Benton Harbor (17 March 1903) to establish the Israelite House of David, Church of the New Eve, Body of Christ, the Seventh Church in the lineage of the Israelite faith, tracing its roots back to the Visitation of Joanna Southcott, at Devonshire, England, 1792.

Joanna Southcott

From 1792 through 1892 would see six Messengers give forth teachings concerning the Second Coming of Christ, its allotted time of preparation for it, and the ingathering of Israel unto this final and great expectation. All six were of English descent, and all began their missions from England. Richard Brothers, a lieutenant in the British navy, was during Joanna Southcott's time, and preceded her by several years, 1790-1792. For his statements regarding the Monarchy and its displacement upon the return of Christ to Earth, Mr. Brothers spend ten years in an English prison as a guest of the Royal family. He is counted as the second Messenger, and the Book of the Revelation to Saint John gives his imprisonment as ten days, in figure (Rev. 2:10); Joanna was instrumental in securing the release of Brothers in 1802.

Joanna Southcott is considered the first of the lineage, and called the "mother" of the Visitation, and became one of histori-

cal note in her Visitation of 22 years (1792-1814). With the death of Joanna in December of 1814, her following, estimated at 150,000, splintered into numerous factions and many would fall away from the faith altogether.

1815 saw the third Messenger, George Turner, a prominent merchant of Leeds, stand up to lead the main bodies of the believers in Joanna; and with his Book of Wonders, 1817, would continue the catalogue of Divine Communications that began with Joanna's 65 volumes taken orally by those of her attendants, Jane Townley and Anne Underwood, who would be with her continually for this very reason. Joanna's history is colourful, as her popularity came to rival the Church of England; for among those that believed on her were men of notable wealth and position, men in Parliament, and clergy from within the Church of England. Though a member of the Church of England, Joanna gave the state Church its day of inquisition; her prophecies, communications, and Biblical interpretations were more widely circulated and read than the Church's doctrine to its own defense. After almost two centuries of misplacement, in 1985, a work was published at the University of Texas Press, authored by James K. Hopkins, which finally gave Joanna her rightful position as one of the major religious figures of influence in England at the beginning of the 19th century.

After all, Joanna held the spotlight for most of the year, 1814, in England and throughout Europe: the headlines were all Joanna, fanning a hysteria from her announced pregnancy in May, to the childbirth and her subsequent death in

December; leaving Napoleon, and the closing hours of the war with America, on page 2.

George Turner was a very early follower of Joanna's teachings, and was to himself receive Communications from 1815-1821, compiling ten published works. Also among the following of Joanna was William Shaw, who resided over a small circle of those that had remained faithful to Joanna; he became the fourth in the lineage of instruments (1821-1822) whose manuscripts would circulate, but remain unpublished until into the 20th century, wherefrom Carpenter's Bookshop in San Diego, California, all six Messengers would be published in their available entirety.

John Wroe

John Wroe began his mission from Bradford, England, 14 December 1822, becoming fifth in the line of Messengers to Israel at the latter day. John's following, though not to the numbers of Joanna, were yet extensive throughout England, Australia, and in America during the time of his 40 years ministry; and unto this day the Christian Israelite Church is represented on three continents, with its headquarters in Australia. John Wroe founded the Society of Christian Israelites and its numerous Church bodies throughout his 40 years of extensive travels; three times he would circle the Earth preaching the Second Coming of Christ, and the restoration of Eden to the Earth. From John Wroe were received 4 decades of Divine Communications adding to the library of volumes now received through five Messengers. John died at Melbourne, Australia, during his third world tour, in 1863; he had prophesied consistently of America: "I have been commanded time after time to go to America;" "The remainder of the song of Moses and the Lamb shall be sent from America;" "Now Son of Man, thou shalt take a light in thy hand and thou shalt go forth into America, and with that light shall the Lord push the people together;" "Prophesy against foreign nations, say, Thus saith the Lord, I have a seed in America, and they shall come by hundreds, fifties, and thousands."

James Jezreel

James White, a once soldier in the British army in India, would become the sixth Messenger with his writing of the Flying Roll, which he submitted to the Trustees of the 5th Church, the Christian Israelites; becoming his petition for their acceptance of a further revelation into the Book that was sealed with seven seals, Revelation chapters 5 and 10. John Wroe had prophesied before his death in 1863, that "a man in the red coat would come in 12 years"; James presented himself before the Trustees of that society in 1875 with the loose leaf writings of the "Flying Roll." The trustees response was to burn the manuscript. Upon which James re-wrote from memory the "Extracts From the Flying Roll," 725 pages; which, with the Old and New Testament volumes, became the doctrinal texts of the New and Latter House of Israel.

Joanna, John Wroe, and James all had their inner circles with attendants, that when the communications would come, they would be recorded. James would give the sign by carrying keys; John Wroe would put on his hat and close his eyes. Most of

Isaiah. Ch. LXV & LXVI.   JOANNA SOUTHCOTT.   Jan.y 1812.

London's most prominent engraver, William Sharp, did this engraving of Joanna Southcott in 1812. Sharp was one of Joanna's earliest within her inner circle. By 1812 her following was nearing the numbers of 100,000 in England and Europe; and there were Joanna imposters which prompted this portrait of her likeness, which today is hung in the British Museum, London.

the volumes of the first six Messengers were recordings written as they were orally given. James would change his name to James Jezreel (Hebrew for the seed of God), and would attract a considerable following in the United Kingdom, Australia, New Zealand, Canada and America. Within his single American tour in 1882, James would make several stops in Michigan, including Grand Rapids, and at Detroit he was recorded as saying, "O blessed Michigan, for out of thee shall come a star". James Jezreel would pass suddenly in 1888, but left the movement with further volumes, and concurring prophecies back to Joanna, declaring the consummation in the Seventh Church with its Messenger. All six taught that there would be seven; John Wroe prophesied that, When thou art at home thou shalt be in America; James spoke directly of Michigan.

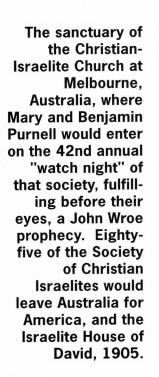

The sanctuary of the Christian-Israelite Church at Melbourne, Australia, where Mary and Benjamin Purnell would enter on the 42nd annual "watch night" of that society, fulfilling before their eyes, a John Wroe prophecy. Eighty-five of the Society of Christian Israelites would leave Australia for America, and the Israelite House of David, 1905.

So it came to pass in the late 1880's that "Extracts" preachers from the New and Latter House of Israel would canvass America thoroughly; and in passing through Richmond, Indiana, in their street preaching style, coast to coast, would catch the ear of the young couple Benjamin and Mary Purnell. The preachers must certainly have impressed the Purnells; Benjamin had received all of his reading education from Bible texts, and from early childhood was often exhibited by his father for his avid ability to preach a moving sermon upon a footstool.

No. 53.   (New Series).

THE
MESSENGER of WISDOM
AND
ISRAEL'S GUIDE.

A PUBLICATION DEVOTED TO THE INGATHERING AND RESTORATION OF THE TWELVE TRIBES OF THE HOUSE OF ISRAEL.

"The Sceptre shall not depart from Judah, nor a Lawgiver from between his feet, until Shiloh come ; and unto him shall the gathering of the People be." Gen. xlix. 10

"I will utter things which have been kept secret from the foundation of the world."
—Matt. xiii. 35.

"The flying roll"

"Take thee again another roll, and write in it all the former words that were in the first roll, which Jehoiakim the king of Judah hath burned."
—Jer. xxxvi. 28.

The New & Latter House of Israel

BOOK DEPOT : 6, BURLINGTON AVENUE, KEW GARDENS, SURREY.

Address of Local Agent :—

Title page of leaflet materials of the sixth Church of James Jezreel, in the 1880s; such flyers that Mary and Benjamin first saw in Richmond, Indiana, around 1888, distributed by the travelling preachers from the New and Latter House of Israel.

Born 27 March 1861 in Greenup, Kentucky, to Madison and Sarah Purnell, Benjamin was the youngest of 12 Purnell children (7th of 7 boys): and at the time of first hearing the preachers of James Jezreel, he was in his late 20s with a wife and two young children. Mary was born 13 November 1862, at Nickelsville, Scott County, Virginia, the daughter of James and Winnod Stallard, she being the 8th of the 12 Stallard children. Their daughter Hettie was yet an infant, born 4 February, 1887, and son, Samuel Coy, was yet a boy, born 28 November 1881. The hearing of the "Extracts" in Richmond near about 1888 would change completely the direction of their lives.

William G. Bulley and his wife Anna came from Melbourne, Australia in 1905. William was a Trustee of the Society of Christian Israelites, with a family lineage in the fifth church back to England of John Wroe's time, 1822-1863. Two of their daughters would walk with Mary into the re-organization of 1930, Jane Ripper and Emma Rowe.

The Purnells were soon to receive copies of the volume of the "Extract From the Flying Roll" for their own examination; and upon reading they began to correspond with the main body at Chatham, England. Addresses and contacts were then established with the numerous subscribers to the Pioneer of Wisdom (the monthly publication of the New and Latter House of Israel) throughout America, as the numbers of believers in America came to rival that of the home bodies in England. Fowlerville, Grand Rapids, and Detroit, Michigan were all homes of circles of New and Latter House members, which were also sources of printed materials sent out from

Chatham. One of their early contacts, and perhaps one in the party that first met the Purnells in Richmond, was Canadian born Michael Mills, then a resident of Detroit. Mills, a preacher himself, would soon establish a communal home in Detroit to which the Purnell family would come in the year 1891. Michael Mills soon recognized the formidable and impressive power of Benjamin Purnell as a preacher, which gave the Purnells the position of traveling with parties throughout mid-America preaching and distributing literature from the New and Latter House of Israel.

1892 would complete the first 100 years from the beginning of Communications received by Joanna Southcott, and 6 Messengers had come forth of the 7 prophesied of, and their respective bodies of believers--Churches. For 3 years Mary and Benjamin would live the communal life after the example in the Book of the Acts of the Apostles, also practicing the austere tenets from the Old Testament sects of the Nazarites and Essenes: vegetarianism, celibacy, uncut hair, abstinence from alcohol and tobacco, and a vow to serve the Lord God of Israel for the life-time. Their time spent at the commune was the time of wintering, as the summer months found them on the road preaching wheresoever they could get an audience; street corner, church, or hall.

Their message in the Extracts sermons was the preparation for the return of Christ to Earth, the beginning of the millennial reign of Christ on Earth; before which time the 7th angel messenger must be found.

And the Seventh angel sounded; and there were

great voices in heaven, saying, The kingdoms of this world are become the kingdoms of our Lord, and of His Christ; and He shall reign forever and ever. Revelation 11:15. But in the days of the voice of the seventh angel, when he shall begin to sound, the mystery of God should be finished, as he hath declared to his servants the prophets. Revelations 10:7.

As the Extracts taught, and the prophecy went accordingly back to Richard Brothers and Joanna, so the Purnells were on the lookout for this 7th messenger to finish the mystery of God, and to complete the heavily quoted number seven.

Detroit, Michigan, 12 March 1895, just 2:00 a.m.; during a late night meeting that lasted into the wee hours, there was a commotion at the Mills communal house. Again an event that would change the course of the little Purnell family forever.

The Substance of the entire 100 years was to be the coming forth of the 7th Messenger, who was to complete the Visitation message that would clearly reveal the mystery of Godliness, God manifest in flesh, from 1 Timothy 3:16; 1 Thessalonians 5:23; Revelation 21:1-4; John 6:44-58. This was to herald forth the time of the end, a time given in which the end would come about predictably, and in a natural way; a time spoken of by Jesus Christ, that would of a necessity be shortened to save

One of the several Baushke families that was first in Benton Harbor to accept Mary and Benjamin as the Seventh Messenger. Both Albert and brother Louis were "Extracts" readers, and within their Benton Harbor carriage shop was built one of the first automobiles in the world.

flesh, and on account of the elect, those days shall be shortened. Matthew 24:22.

On that morning of the 12th day of March, 1895, Mary and Benjamin found themselves, in fact, the covenanted receivers of the seventh anointing, called Shiloh-Immanuel, the substance of 6 prophetic messengers in the history of the first 100 years.

The name Shiloh is Hebrew from the Old Testament: in the 49th chapter of Genesis Jacob calls his sons together and prophesies unto them of that which should, "befall you in the latter days." He tells them that Judah would hold the sceptre of the Law until Shiloh come; and unto him shall the gathering of the people be, verse 10. History has now proven this prophecy, for indeed Judah has persevered with the sceptre of the Law by which they have remained the only family of the 12 sons of Jacob recognizable unto the latter day, by reason of their maintenance of the custom and commandment out of the Law.

Shiloh is to be the embodiment of the spirit of truth, in the person of the 7th messenger to create the setting for the gathering of the elect of the family of Israel, and to give instruction for the preparation of the coming kingdom of Christ on Earth.

Now we beseech you, brethren, by the coming of our Lord Jesus Christ, and by our gathering together unto Him, That ye be not soon shaken in mind, or be troubled, neither by spirit, nor by word, nor by letter as from us, as that the day of Christ is at hand.
2 Thessalonians 2:1 and 2; Matthew 24:31.

Benjamin received communications later that very day, and the dynamics of the group at Detroit changed literally overnight. At first there was acceptance and support for the young Purnell couple, which within weeks changed to that of jealousies and strivings to undermine the experience that most of the entire household had witnessed. As Spring broke, Mary and Benjamin, with Hettie now 8, and Coy 14, departed from Detroit, never to return; with hearts broken by love so accepting and warm, now turned to spite, that was even leveled at the children. With nowhere to call home, 2 children to feed and protect, Mary and Benjamin began their 6 years of sojourning throughout mid-America, during which time the Star of Bethlehem, The Living Roll of Life, 780 pages would be written as received, through Benjamin Purnell.

Baushke Brothers Carriage Shop, 1912. Several of the number of Baushke families in the Benton Harbor area joined the Israelite House of David in the beginning years, comprising a noticeable portion of the membership, 1903-1905. Another early comer to the House of David, upon getting a tour and meeting many of the folks around the colony, would ask his tour guide, Benjamin Purnell, "Brother Benjamin, was Abraham's name Baushke?"

The little Purnell family travelled south into Ohio, and then all across the 4 state area of Kentucky, Indiana, Illinois, and Ohio for 6 years walking, biking, catching train rides; and last of all they were able to obtain a wagon and 2 horses. The itinerant life as a travelling preacher is not one of wealth or comforts; along with the love and providence for 2 children, and without a home base surrounding, it makes for a very difficult answer as to a means to survive. But Providence it surely was for them: "One time we were travelling, trying to make it to the next town where we could hold meeting that night, and Benjamin was not well, and he laid down on some railroad ties by the roadside. I said to him I did not think we could make it to the town that night. On one side of the road there was a row of houses and on the other side was a thick woods, and I said to Benjamin, I will go up to one of these houses and get a room. Benjamin said, No, I will tell you where to go. Walk right along down this road until you come to a road leading right through the thick woods, and follow that road until you come to a white house, and the lady there will keep us, for I heard her voice saying twice: "I will keep you". So I followed his instructions and I came to the white house and went to the door and rapped, and a lady came out, and I explained our mission, that we were travelling preachers, and I told her it was getting late and could we get a room with her overnight. She said, "Yes, I will keep you." Then I said, My brother is not well, could you keep him also? She said, "Yes, I will keep you".

During their 6 years of travel they were able to get speaking engagements with donations that provided no more than the necessities, but most valuable were the hundreds of interested parties with whom a correspondence they would keep; and through a kind offering Mary and Benjamin were able to publish a series of short tracts, which gave an outline of the Israelite faith. These they handed out in volume where ever they went to hold meetings, open air, or churches. By 1902 they had found a home among a few families of believers in Fostoria, Ohio, and the manuscript of the "Star of Bethlehem" would be completed and published in its first edition at Ashland, Ohio. Numerous were the names of those who were in contact with the small circle at Fostoria; through personal meetings with Mary and Benjamin, these corresponded asking for copies of the Star of Bethlehem as soon as it was printed, and directions as to where and when the gathering would begin.

By January 1903 the Star of Bethlehem was in the hands of many throughout mid-America, which stated that the gathering would begin in that same year, and there were those that wanted to come immediately to Fostoria to join the Israelite House of David. It has come down by way of mouth that Mary Purnell was given the Communication of the name Benton Harbor, to which no one at the Fostoria circle had ever heard of. Upon finding it on the map, and that it was near the Lake area, Benjamin Purnell was to have exclaimed that God was Bent on Harboring His People. So the small party of eight from the Fostoria area, being Silas, his wife Cora, their son Paul Mooney; John Schneider, Charles Norris, Mary, Benjamin, and Hettie Purnell, made plans to leave towards the first week in March with the breaking of Spring. Samuel Coy has left home already on his own, being 22, and Hettie would turn 16 on 4 February.

"From Mary and Benjamin's Travels"

"Then one time I remember well, we went to the trustees of a church and got permission to hold a meeting there, and we went from house to house and advertised our meeting. The preacher who preached in this church lived in the country, and the trustees said it would be alright, for he seldom ever preached there. So that night as the crowd was about gathered, and the house was packed, he sent us word that he would preach there himself. Well, we went up and he was sitting in the pulpit. We walked straight down the aisle to the pulpit, and turning around faced the audience and said, 'You have all gathered to hear us speak, so we want to tell you that we will now preach on the street,' and we walked straight out and it emptied the house and left him in the pulpit alone. We preached on that street corner to a very large crowd, and they treated us fine.

One day we were walking along with our hair flowing in the breeze and passed a field full of horses and cattle and they all came to the fence and looked over so wistfully at us. Some of them put their heads over and looked as far as they could see us. It was a peculiar thing.

We came into a town once and preached on the street, then went into a store and the people crowded around and looked very serious. The next day a man came up to our camp and said, 'Did you notice the crowd around the store?' We said, 'Yes.' He said, 'Well they said you folks did not belong here, you surely were from another planet.' Once we came into a town-- that was when we were walking, and two little boys ran to their mother and said, 'Surely one was Jesus and the other God,' and she said, 'I suppose they are showmen' and the boys said, 'No, they have good faces.'

Many many times we went without food, but not once did we ever ask for anything to eat, for we believed as the Psalmist David said, 'I have been young and now I am old, yet I have never seen the righteous forsaken nor His seed begging bread,' and how wonderfully have we seen the great hand of God that fed us. We have called at different places in the afternoon at 3:00 o'clock, or later, and asked for a drink of water and the lady of the house would set food on the table and have us go to her dining room and eat; for which we always felt so thankful to the God of Israel, knowing that He who watched over us neither slumbered nor slept, and we were never discouraged, knowing that He knew the things we stood in need of before we asked."

Mary Stallard and Benjamin Purnell's marriage certificate August 29, 1880, Aberdeen, Ohio

Benjamin Franklin Purnell 1885 at age 24

Hettie Purnell, as a child, would spend 7 of her 16 years on the road, or staying with friends and relations of Mary and Benjamin, from age 5 through 15. Her mother would keep a number of her little Hettie's photographs close to her for all the 50 years that she would live in the Israelite community at Benton Harbor.

As Mary and Benjamin left Detroit with broken hearts and the bitter taste of malice and jealousy at their backs, so before their departure from Fostoria they would be devastated by the sudden loss of their beautiful young daughter, Hettie. 18 February 1903, Hettie's first day at work in a fireworks factory in Fostoria ended in the ultimate tragedy of an explosion and consequent fire that killed all within the factory. Burned beyond recognition; only by the ring upon Hettie's finger, a gift from Cora Mooney just 2 weeks earlier for her birthday, were they able to identify the charred remains.

Her mother, already weak with an ongoing illness of several years, was brought down to near nothing; while Benjamin addressed the cynics of their message with words of apology for being unable to attend his daughter's funeral, and Thanksgiving towards all that sent cards and gifts to the Purnells in sympathy for their tragic loss.

By the end of 2 weeks the small circle of now seven would depart from Fostoria for Benton Harbor, Michigan; the father solemn with his loss, and the mother still with her compounded illness from 6 years on the road. Faith that was longsuffering as it was unquenchable in the Purnells brought them to a new beginning at the mouth of the Saint Joseph River, on Lake Michigan by 17 March 1903.

Hettie Purnell

Hettie photographed at her 16th birthday, only 2 weeks before her death.

Mary with her only son Samuel Coy, at the House of David; Coy would never take an interest in his parent's life work, and at times would be a bit of an embarrassment to their austere principles of living.

April 6, 1903

> Sunday afternoon and evening services were held at the Armory by the newly formed House of Israel, the newly arrived sect of Second Adventists. Addresses were made by the leaders, Benjamin and Mary.

Israelite
House of David
1903

Israelite families at the House of David, 1907.

Immediately upon arrival in Benton Harbor, Mary and Benjamin made arrangements for public meetings in and throughout the town, and advertising the same. Among those quick to take interest was the Albert Baushke family of the Baushke Brothers, well-to-do carriage makers, and builders of one of the very first automobiles in the world. Several in the number of Baushke families were soon to join in with the band of 7; Albert himself was a James Jezreel adherent and a believer in the teachings of the Extracts from the Flying Roll. By early April came those who had petitioned Mary and Benjamin while yet at Fostoria, and the numbers grew quickly. Most all of the first arrivals were former followers of James Jezreel, and upon reading the Star of Bethlehem accepted Mary and Benjamin as the Seventh Messenger for which many were on the lookout. The headquarters of the Christian Israelites at Melbourne, Australia, also

received a copy of the Star of Bethlehem in 1903, which secretly caused quite a stir. John had prophesied that within 42 years the 7th would come forth. In October of 1904 Mary and Benjamin, their son Coy, and a small party embarked on their only round the world mission via Melbourne, Australia. Arriving in Melbourne around Christmas of 1904, they petitioned the Trustees of the Church for an audience. Every January from John Wroe's death of that same month in 1863, the Society held an annual "watch night"; 42 years later Mary and Benjamin would enter the Church of the main body to announce the beginnings of the 7th Church at Benton Harbor. After a stormy reception, silence fell to hear a resounding sermon given by Benjamin that convinced 85 of that assembly, among whom were notables of lineage in the Church, and two Trustees. Indeed a tumultuous shake up, as an impressive and integral part of the main body at Melbourne departed with Mary and Benjamin west-

Arrival of 85 Australians
at Benton Harbor,
Bound for the House of David.
March 27th 1905.

ward through the Indian Ocean enroute to their 27 March landing in New York, Benjamin's 44th birthday, 1905.

The foundation of the Israelite House of David was made up of both 5th and 6th Church members, and new interest was growing so rapidly that the Church would advertise in the monthly paper published at the colony for folks not to come before they were called, as houses could not be built fast enough to accommodate all that were coming. Demand for the Star of Bethlehem had already absorbed the first edition, and in late 1903 a second edition was printed on the Israelite presses. By 1907 there were over 700 members of the Israelite community; more land was needed, more homes to be built, and new sources of income explored in order to feed, clothe, and house this population, with more wanting to come in. Preachers were sent out throughout America and Canada, the United Kingdom, Australia and New Zealand, where Branches were established at London and Sydney, Australia.

Famous photograph of the parade of the 85 Australians along Water Street enroute to the House of David, 1905.

1906 "Bethlehem" completed and "Jerusalem" under construction along Britain Avenue. Israelite architects designed and Israelite carpenters built all of the buildings on Britain Avenue and the Eden Springs property. Berrien County suspiciously watched in amazement.

1908 saw the amusement park open to help answer the income problems; by 1913 whiskers, and long hair were playing music and baseball across the continent to the delight of the whole country. Incomes were readily coming in; the gathering was still growing with new properties and businesses; and Benton Harbor was known worldwide as the home of the Israelite House of David. By 1916 the numbers of those gathered at home hovered 1000; southwestern Michigan prospered in the wealth of products and tourism the colony had brought to it.

Over the years just preceding the first world-war, and after, the Israelites would send out business parties to Chicago and northern Indiana cities to advertise Benton Harbor as THE vacation spot in the midwest for the summer months. The numerous agricultural enterprises from at least 10 farms were the backbone of the quantities, and quality that made the Benton Harbor Fruit Market the largest open air market in the world.

The well-being of prosperity and fame would continue to follow Mary and Benjamin through the World War and into the first years of the "Roaring Twenties"; jazz was hot, and the Israelites produced 2 traveling bands that played with the best of them, from L.A. and New Orleans, to the Cotton Club. But back home the band was playing "The House of David Blues."

1907 - 1908
Eden Springs of
The House of David

Mary and Benjamin Purnell, 1907; a year that saw Israelite preachers encompass most of the English speaking, western world, while the number at home grew to 700. George Wheeler would walk with his family from Arkansas, pushing a cart of family belongings, and preaching from town to town as they came to Benton Harbor, Michigan.

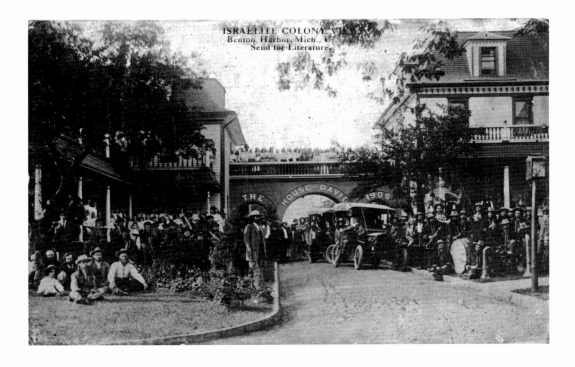

1907--Departure of First Preacher's Tours by automobile.

1907--Sunday afternoon at the original ice cream parlour to the north of "Bethlehem" and "Jerusalem" buildings.

1907--Israelite preachers that would circle the planet with the message of the coming millennial reign of Christ on earth.

AUSTRALIA

HEADQUARTERS:

LIVERPOOL ROAD, ENFIELD, SYDNEY, N. S. WALES
698 BRUNSWICK ST., FITZROY, MELBOURNE, VICTORIA

AGENTS FOR ISRAEL'S LITERATURE:

N. S. WALES BOOKSTALL CO., 476 GEORGE STREET, SYDNEY.
E. V. COLE, BOOK ARCADE, BOURKE ST., MELBOURNE, VIC.

Enfield, Sydney, N. S. W.

YOUR last notes and letters have been received, and as usual, we were glad to hear from home again; and we were also glad to learn of the success this season, and of the large crowds visiting the colony.

This last month the weather has been very much unsettled. We were only able to hold one meeting in the Domain. However this meeting was fairly well attended. We are looking forward to the time when we will be able to do more in the spiritual line. The brothers and sisters out in the field report good success.

The case of literature containing the Special Souvenir SHILOH'S MESSENGER OF WISDOM edition has been received, and the contents were much enjoyed. Already we have sent out a good supply to the workers in the field, so that those who are in the famine, and have the opportunity of hearing the words of the Lord rightly divided, can get their sacks filled with the good old and new corn of the land.

In the days of old the children of Israel went down into Egypt to get their sacks filled with corn the second time; and now we have the Second Child. And when the search went round, the silver cup was found in the mouth of the sack of the younger brother; and they could not get more corn except the younger brother be with them. And when they were brought before Joseph, they were tested strongly; and when he was revealed to them they went and brought the rest of the family quickly. And it is written, The thing that has been, shall be again; for we must have our younger brother with us in order to have our sacks filled the second time. And as he who had the silver cup in his sack's mouth was taken, so now there will be 144,000 taken and ever be with the Lord. Therefore the Second Child who stands up in his stead shall rule all nations with a rod of iron (the spirit). And all of the living are considered with him. And so it is also written, When the Son of man shall come, before him shall all nations be gathered, and, Unto Shiloh shall the gathering of the people be; and, In the days of the voice of the seventh angel, when he shall begin to sound, the mystery shall be finished as declared to his servants the prophets. Rev. 10-7.

The twelve tribes are to be redeemed from among men, and live and reign here upon this earth, and he will give them a white stone, and in it a new name which none knoweth save those who receive it. And they will keep the virgin law of life—the same law which Jesus kept—which law will free us from the law of sin and death; riding triumphantly over sin, death, hell and the grave—delivered from the bondage of corruption into the glorious liberty of the children of God; having their vile bodies changed and fashioned like unto his glorious body. This will bring the kingdom down here on earth—"Thy will be done in earth, as it was done in heaven;" and the meek shall inherit the earth (body), for this mortal shall put on immortality.

JOHNNIE.

1907 (left to right) Cora Mooney, Mary, Benjamin, Edith Meldrim, Lillian Hannaford, Florence Tulk, Ada Ross and Rachel Hannaford

Music became synonymous with The House of David for half a century.

1907--Benjamin, Mary and Cora Mooney foreground--first automobile in center; girls band to the right. Photo taken along Britain Avenue frontage by Israelite photographer Harry Kirkham.

ENGLAND AND WALES

HEADQUARTERS: 16 Nelson Street, E. London.

Birmingham, England, April 30, '07.

The year and month are both closing with to-day, so we write home. We have spent the most of April in Birmingham. Many good meetings have been held here in the "Bull Ring," a market centre of Birmingham. We have had much to be glad of in seeing eight Extract believers eagerly reading the Star of Bethlehem. Seven of them are full members of the Sixth Church. All are progressing very favorably so far. Brother and Sister H— are convinced that the Star is the truth. Brother U— said Sunday, I don't know what you are going to do, but I shall first give this message to all my friends, then I shall settle up my business and go. I will not ask any man's opinion nor stop to confer with flesh and blood. We have heard of seven others near here to whom we will give the message. So far Maxwell has been having a one-sided game over here. He has warned his flock against the Star. One Brother had formed such a poor opinion of the House of David that he first declared he would not read a thing. But by bowing to reason and proving all things he now has the four Stars and is delighted; and says, "Its just the people I have been looking for."

Strange to say these seven members have all lived celebate lives for several years, having been convinced all Israel must come to that. They thought the Extracts plain on that line. Some of them have been vegetarians also. They were certainly prepared to receive the Seventh Message and said they were expecting it to come. We hope to see them all well grounded in the faith. Then we hope to go north where we have heard of other members. When Sister H— saw us preaching she said she thought the seventy preachers may have gone out with their hair down. Brother I —and Brother O — and two sons are about ready to go out in their van or carriage. It is a fine car, all wood. The roads in England are all paved so they will not have mud roads. They may start May 6th.

Saturday evening we had Brother H—'s assistance at the meetings. He takes a delight in preaching. All the members are active workers, both in natural as well as spiritual things. They are healthy and sound minded. Many have written long, earnest and pathetic letters to John M— and Ann R— without a word of reply, even though money and stamps were sent. This has occured a great many times. Then he quotes "feed my sheep." John M— told Brother U— some time ago he should not live a celebate life because you are neither bringing forth fruit for the Lord nor the devil. However if the Star of Bethlehem ever gets among his people it will divide the sheep from the goats. When God speaks all men are silent. We are very glad John has been used to scatter the Extracts and to gather some members in bodies here and there, so we cannot complain. Brother U— has a great desire to preach and hopes to be a great helper. We met many who have the Extracts around here but are not followers

BIRDIE AND DAVID.

ISRAELITE COLONY VIEW
Benton Harbor, Mich., U. S. A.
Send for literature.

The cart shown in the above picture was pushed by George Wheeler and family a distance of 1200 miles on their way to the ingathering of Israel at Benton Harbor

Benjamin Purnell would do two portraits, one of Jesus Christ, and the other, his wife Mary, (above) done in pencil, chalk, and crayon. Benjamin Purnell would write, and publish 2 books of poetry, along with many unpublished pieces; he did numerous landscapes in vivid pastels; he wrote 41 Dialogues, including "the Prince of Peace," and "Joseph in Egypt" plays. He made the formula for the diamond sparkling stones in the Diamond House and Mary's Hotel constructions; he would write and publish 4 volumes of the Star of Bethlehem, 7 Books of Wisdom, 6 volumes of Balls of Fire, and numerous other articles and essays that would appear in the Shiloh Messenger of Wisdom, 1903 through 1926. Benjamin Purnell would get baseball rolling in the House of David, start a girls athletic program, along with female musical ensembles for voice and instrument. Being ahead of his time in many respects, such as structuring the community and governing

that gave women an equal voice, as in 4 Pillars both male and female, and 12 of the Advisory Board, both numbers male and female. Women could vote and hold office, or run a business in the Israelite House of David in 1903. Health foods and protein vegetarian supplements were first served in Berrien County at the Eden Springs Park Restaurant in 1908. He would foretell that more would convert to vegetarians because meat quality would become so poor; more for this reason than for religious doctrine.

He voiced Temperance over Prohibition, because the mob and big money would more readily capitalize on the Dry. He would write to President Woodrow Wilson, in which letter he would warn of the Japanese imperialism in the Pacific. He would foretell of global warming in 1916; and in 1910 his Israelite colony was the cutting edge on the Religion Page across the country, as a model of efficiency and productivity that put Benton Harbor on the map.

[From the Detroit (Mich.) Tribune.]

BERRIEN COUNTY ADMIRES ISRAELITES FOR THEIR THRIFT AND GENTLENESS

In the picture is shown the House of David, near Benton Harbor, where arrivals from Australia were welcomed one day this week. Fertile fields surround these substantial and commodious dwellings, some of the best cultivated land in Berrien county. The long-haired people of the House of David now own vast tracks of such territory in and about Benton Harbor. Fruit trees and ornamental hedges, with beds of flowers, in season, adorn their lands. The grounds surrounding the headquarters are typical of all their territory.

Benton Harbor merchants are glad to welcome the recruits of the Israelites who are gathering in this city. The feeling that existed toward the long-haired colony when they first began to assemble here, four years ago, has passed away, and the citizens now welcome the Israelites as heartily as they do any other class of newcomers. Since Benjamin and Mary first began to concentrate their forces here, the property in the vicinity of the House of David has seen a wonderful advance. They have purchased some of the finest farms in the county until they have nearly 1,000 acres of fruit land. They have constructed new buildings at an aggregate cost of $75,000 and made numerous improvements on their farms.

The Israelites are peaceable and law-abiding citizens and are among the best customers of the local merchants. All the dry goods, clothing, hardware and supplies that are used at the colony are purchased so far as possible of local dealers.

From the score of members who came here four years ago with Benjamin and Mary and and were crowded into one house they have expanded and now have half a dozen large buildings on their farm nearest the city. Recently the second installment of Australians arrived direct from Melbourne. There were 21 in this party, including men women and children. They were the advance guard of a much larger body who expect to come later.

Some of their best preachers will leave this week for Australia, where they expect to gather together the scattered tribes of Israel. There are known to be several hundred of the Children in the provinces of Australia who are almost ready to come to Benton Harbor.

The Australians who arrived last spring are delighted with America and Americans. They were largely farmers and have devoted themselves to fruit growing. From one farm in Berrien county last fall the Israelites marketed $1,000 worth of peaches each day for four consecutive days. They are equally successful in the growth of corn, oats, beans, potatoes and all vegetables. Their farms are models of neatness and beauty. Chas. Schutz, the real estate agent for the colony, was formerly a fruit commission merchant of this city. Not one dollar's worth of fruit is allowed to go to waste. They have a large evaporator for drying fruit and a canning factory with a large capacity.

Every member of the colony is industrious. There is work for every man, woman and child on the farms or in the shops. The industries operated by the Israelites are numerous. Among them are a black-smith shop, a planing mill and a well equipped printing plant, where their monthly paper, Shiloh's Messenger of Wisdom, with several thousand circulation is published and all their tracts are printed. Their bakery is a model plant. They have their own electric light plant and water works; a fine factory for turning out concrete blocks with which their buildings will be constructed hereafter; a fine green-house, and various other institutions, including a wagon and carriage shop. The colony boasts of two fine brass bands which came from Australia last spring, and one of the best orchestras in the vicinity. Every profession and trade is represented in their ranks.

All their buildings are designed and planned by their own architect and all the work done by their own members. They have a number of fine artists and the interior decorations of their new auditorium is a beautiful piece of work.

The main auditorium will seat about 1,000 people, and will be used for all their religious meetings, which are open to the public.

They are practical socialists. They all live from a common fund. Benjamin foots the bills for all. The weak or infirm are not compelled to work. Their zoo contains many kinds of rare wild animals, which were brought from the country across the waters. The Israelites are strict vegetarians. They use no meats or fish of any description, neither lard. They do not beleive in the taking of any form of life. Instead of lard they use cotton seed oil.

The copyright on the Star of Bethlehem was Mary and Benjamin, and in 1910 it would go into its third edition, following a printshop fire in 1907 that destroyed most of the second edition. By 1910 the Israelite House of David had grown to a world wide fame in its rapid growth, innovative community organization and a fresh and singular view of the doctrine of Jesus Christ. By 1916 there were 1000 at home with hundreds abroad in correspondence.

IMPORTANT NOTICE

OWING to the desire of many to come to the House of David faster than we are able to build and prepare places for them, we wish it understood by all such, that in order to save us and themselves much unnecessary trouble, they should correspond with us before making arrangements to come.

It is absolutely necessary that each and every case be given due consideration and the applicant await for the call to come home, as there must be order in the Lord's house.

A notice that was run continuously in the monthly Shiloh Messenger of Wisdom, from 1906-07 through the first World War.

AN ANIMATED SCENE IN THE ISRAELITES' NEW PARK--VIEW OF ENTRANCE

MARY AND BENJAMIN PURNELL

From a vast marshy swamp to a fine public park, is the story of the transformation of thirty acres of wild land by the House of David association.

Citizens of Benton Harbor and Berrien county would scarcely believe, had they visited the place less than a year so, that it was possible to make such a vast improvement. As improvement that without cost affords a place of amusement and recreation for ten thousand people. Strange as it may seem, nevertheless it is so and the park speaks for itself. Lighted by hundreds of electric lights, furnished with a large amphitheatre, with rustic benches, bridges and driveways and a large lagoon in the centre and twelve different kinds of mineral water flowing from as many fountains, the park during the past month has been visited by thousands of resorters and Benton Harbor people.

The park adjoins Eastman Springs being the west thirty acres and south of Britain avenue. The land was purchased of the Eastman Springs company last summer and work commenced on the improvement at once.

Greening Brothers, the well known nurserymen and experienced landscape gardeners, laid out the grounds. Thousands of plants and shrubs were purchased, each one being marked and numbered for its particular location.

A fine arched entrance leads to the main amusement and summer meeting place. A magnificent cement, dining refreshment and residence hall has been constructed, where meals are served, strictly of a vegetarian nature. Several other small buildings for the comfort of the park have also been constructed.

A depot has been built on Britain avenue where passengers and signals from the street cars and interurban can stop to take the small scenic railway to the main park. The railway is about a mile in length and runs over a high bridge across a ravine three hundred feet long, to Eastman Springs resort. Later the railroad will be extended beyond to Empire avenue, where it is proposed to build a large lake.

On the northeast side of the park is being constructed the animal quarters, in which when completed will be housed the numerous wild animals owned by the association and places also will be built for the vast collection of Australian birds. The quarters are being so constructed that the animals and birds will have running water all the time.

The association recently purchased a number of deer and south of the animal quarters a large park will be built for the deer.

It is the intention of the association to make the place as attractive as the White City in Chicago. When the lake is completed and the scenic railway extended it will be possible to go in and out of the park by boat and rail. More cement walks will be laid and additional archways constructed. Next year a large summer hotel will also be added. More arches for the railway will be built. The refreshment parlor is very attractive and clean, the main counter being built in the shape of a horseshoe and presided over by young ladies, members of the colony. Here soft drinks of all kinds are served, including fancy ice cream dishes. Last Monday the dining hall the following menu was served at the prices given:

Vegetable soup, 10 cents

Specials

Young sugar beets in cream 10c
Stewed tomatoes 10c and corn 10c
Young onions 5c   Lettuce 5c
Peas, 10c, French and stewed
Potatoes, 10c, in cream, mashed, French fried, chip, shoestrings, cottage fried, Juliene, German fried. Augratin 15c.
Eggs 10c, fried, boiled, scrambled, poached, sheared; Augratin 15c.
Omelets, plain and savory, 15c and up
Pancakes 15c   Salads 15c   Cheese 5c

Dessert.
Pies 5c   Assorted cakes 5c   Fruits
Raspberries in cream 15c
Sliced oranges 10c
Coffee 5c   Tea 5c   Milk 5c

Cocoa or chocolate 10c.

Some idea of the number of persons who visit the park may be gained from the fact that last Sunday over twelve hundred passengers were carried on the scenic railway and it is estimated during the day over five thousand people passed through the grounds. Many persons came to drink in the mineral water from the natural springs that supply the fountains. Five bands furnished music throughout the day. The morning exercises opened with music by the bands. This was followed by speaking from Mary and Benjamin, also by other brothers of the House of David.

The growth and development of the House of David is quite remarkable, considering the short time of five years ago when Mary and Benjamin, the leaders, first came to Benton Harbor.

Brother Tyler, president of the association, was one of the first arrivals at the new colony. He was followed by other members who came from all parts of the world to be saved in the faith and the association now numbers between five and six hundred persons.

Speaking of the association Brother Tyler said:

"We started in a rented house and we had faith we would succeed. With Mary and Benjamin as leaders, taking the scriptures as our guide, we ever will succeed."

The first permanent building known as the House of David was built the same year. The building contained about thirty rooms, with a printing plant in the basement. Shortly afterwards becoming crowded for quarters another building of fifty rooms was constructed on Britain avenue, and shortly afterwards another house adjoining this of sixty rooms was built. Later a separate printing plant was built. Soon a power house, laundry building and work shops were added. About three years ago the zoological gardens were started, and now the gardens contain a vast collection of animals and birds, including wolves, foxes, bears, coons, etc. and many rare birds from Australia.

Many of the members of the colony are expert agriculturists and the association has some of the finest farms in the township. Starting with five acres they have kept adding to their original until now they own several hundred acres.

About eighteen months ago the association commenced the construction of the first concrete and stone building and since then have added several new concrete buildings which will be the office building and general headquarters.

Fire destroyed the frame printing plant also the power plant. Immediately plans were made for a fire proof printing, electric lights and power plant with a floor space of about three times larger than the one that burned. This was completed about a year ago.

The association raise more farm products than they consume. They have a large chicken farm with several thousand chickens, which they raise for laying purposes. The eggs they eat and sell.

The October freeze of two years ago damaged their peach orchards considerably. However, they immediately began replanting the orchards and also set out considerable small fruit.

While looking after their material welfare the association never neglects its spiritual advancement, and the members never fail to impress upon an inquirer the hope of immortal life.

HOUSE OF DAVID ISRAELITE GROUNDS--VIEW OF COLONY'S QUARTERS

An Israelite Character

An interesting member of the colony is Brother James D. Tucker. Standing about six feet tall with keen, sharp brown eyes, Mr. Tucker would attract attention in most any crowd of men. His bearing is that of a gentleman in every respect, and his conversation is marked by well chosen words and grammatical sentences.

Mr. Tucker, who is one of the spiritual advisers, in speaking of their coming said—

YOUR PIANO IS HERE.

Among the recent large shipment of pianos to this store were some beauties. We have one for you.

Fine New Chase, Hackley and Bush & Lane Pianos at Special Prices. We also handle Victor Graphophones and Edison Phonographs and records.

B. R. CASE & CO.

Masonic Temple, St. Joseph, Next Door to Interurban Station.

IS YOUR HOUSE WIRED?

Electric Breezes

Where's the sense in wasting your strength and patience trying to battle with the heat?

What's the use of placing your entire nervous system in jeopardy by trying to do your work, look pleasant, and be pleasant when you're sweltering?

It's false economy, when all that's necessary is the proper distribution of ELECTRIC FANS about your home, store, office, or factory.

Where's the economy in telling employes to waste two or three hours every day, popping beers, changing collars, shifting positions to get air, and taking occasional trips to the thirst parlors?

THERE IS NONE

Electric breezes from ELECTRIC FANS transform the place into a veritable paradise during dog days.

The cost is practically nothing in comparison with the comfort and enjoyment realized.

BENTON HARBOR-ST. JOSEPH RAILWAY & LIGHT CO., Telephone 281

BALKED IN CRUSADE

CHARLOTTE MAYOR FAILS IN EFFORT TO STOP SUNDAY BALL.

Executive Yells For Game to Halt, But Is Not Heeded.

Special to The News-Palladium.

Charlotte, Mich., July 20.—Early Sunday morning Mayor Tobbs posted placards in business parts of town, stating that Sunday baseball was strictly forbidden. The largest crowd that ever saw a game at Bennett park was present at 3 o'clock when two local teams composed of factory men started to play to test the question. In the second inning Mayor Tobbs asked the crowd to disperse or the mayor would place the players under arrest.

The players paid no heed to the mayor and Officer Halladay stepped to the home plate and told the players that if the game was continued the players could consider themselves under arrest. At this point Attorney G. C. Fox stepped out of his automobile into the diamond and informed the players that Mr. Halladay or no other officer, could arrest them without a warrant, and told them to resist arrest and proceed with the game, which advice was followed.

No arrests were made yesterday, but it is expected that both teams will be brought into court today. It is expected that warrants for Sunday observance violators will be thick and fast if any of the ball players are convicted. Six of the eight aldermen were present, Alderman Moll acting as umpire.

NEW ADMINISTRATION BUILDING

THE FEEDING OF CHILDREN

Receives Far More Care and Intelligent Study Than Formerly.

It used to be that even educated people devoted more attention to their children's morals than to their health. Happily, we are becoming more enlightened and in the family of the day laborer as in that of the scholar the child's physical needs are conscientiously studied, and an effort is made to build young constitutions in the right way.

It goes without saying that no question in the rearing of children is more important than the method of preparation of the breakfast food he gives his children. Cereals are great fuel for the little furnaces, if the starch—70 per cent of wheat—has been broken up by heat so the digestive juices can get at it.

The Hygienic Food Company of Battle Creek, Mich., is the organization that has gone into this matter thoroughly. Its product—Mapl-Flake—will serves as an illustration of how cereal food should be prepared for children. The Blue Washington wheat used in Mapl-Flake is steam cooked for six hours, then crisp Each kernel is flaked so that the digestive juices can reach it and the starch is thoroughly cooked.

OLD RESIDENT OF HAGAR DIES SUNDAY

Mrs. Isaac Farnum, a long resident of Hagar, died Sunday morning at 8 o'clock, after being ill with cancer. She leaves a husband, a son and a daughter, besides a sister, Mrs. M. L. Ferry of this city and a half sister, Mrs. W. Ryno, also of this city, a mother, Mrs. Roswell Curtis, residing in Hagar and a brother Addie Allen, of Coloma. The funeral services will be held at the house Tuesday afternoon at 2 o'clock.

From a vast marshy swamp to a fine public park, is the story of the transformation of thirty acres of wild land by the House of David association.

Citizens of Benton Harbor and Berrien county would scarcely believe, had they visited the place less than a year ao, that it was possible to make such a vast improvement. An improvement that without cost affords a place of amusement and recreation for ten thousand people. Strange as it may seem, nevertheless it is so and the park speaks for itself. Lighted by hundreds of electric lights, furnished with a large amphitheatre, with rustic benches, bridges and driveways and a large lagoon in the centre and twelve different kinds of mineral water flowing from as many fountains, the park during the past month has been visited by thousands of resorters and Benton Harbor people.

The park adjoins Eastman Springs being the west thirty acres and south of Britain avenue. The land was purchased of the Eastman Springs company last summer and work commenced on the improvement at once.

Greening Brothers, the well known nurserymen and experienced landscape gardners, laid out the grounds. Thousands of plants and shrubs were purchased, each one being marked and numbered for its particular location.

A fine arched entrance leads to the main amusement and summer meeting place. A magnificent cement, dining, refreshment and residence hall has been constructed, where meals are served, strictly of a vegetarian nature. Several other small buildings for the comfort of the park have also been constructed.

A depot has been built on Britain avenue where passengers and sightseers from the street cars and interurban can stop to take the small scenic railway to the main park. The railway is about a mile in length and runs over a high bridge across a ravine three hundred feet long, to Ravina Springs resort. Later the railroad will be extended beyond to Empire avenue, where it is proposed to build a large lake.

On the northeast side of the park is being constructed the animal quarters, in which when completed will be housed the numerous wild animals owned by the association and places also will be built for the vast collection of Australian birds. The quarters are being so constructed that the animals and birds will have running water all the time.

The association recently purchased a number of deer and south of the animal quarters a large park will be built for the deer.

It is the intention of the association to make the place as attractive as the White City in Chicago. When the lake is completed and the scenic railway extended it will be possible to go in and out of the park by boat and rail. More cement walks will be laid and additional archways constructed. Next year a large summer hotel will also be added. More arches for the railway will be built. The refreshment parlor is very attractive and clean, the main counter being built in the shape of a horseshoe and presided over by young ladies, members of the colony. Here soft drinks of all kinds are served, including fancy ice cream dishes. Last Monday at the dining hall the following menu was served at the prices given:

Vegetable soup, 10 cents

Specials.

Young sugar beets in cream 10c
Stewed tomatoes 10c and corn 10c
Young onions 5c   Lettuce 5c
Beans 10, boiled and baked
Peas, 10c, French and stewed
Potatoes, 10c, in cream, mashed,
Frnech fried, chip, shoestrings, cottage fried, liniere, German fried,
Augratin 15c.
Eggs 15c, fried, boiled, scrambled, poached, sheared; Augratin, 15c.
Omelets, plain and savory, 15c and up
Pancakes 15c   Salads 15c   Cheese 5c

Dessert.

Pies 5c   Assorted cakes 5c   Fruits
Raspberries in cream 15c
Sliced oranges 10c
Coffee 5c   Tea 5c   Milk 5c
Cocoa or chocolate 10c.

Some idea of the number of persons who visit the park may be gained from the fact that last Sunday over twelve hundred passengers were carried on the scenic railway and it is estimated during the day over five thousand people passed through the grounds. Many persons came to drink the mineral water from the natural springs that supply the fountains. Five bands furnished music throughout the day. The morning exercises opened with music by the bands. This was followed by speaking from Mary and Benjamin, also by other brothers of the House of David.

The growth and development of the House of David is quite remarkable, considering the short time of five years ago when Mary and Benjamin, the leaders, first came to Benton Harbor.

Brother Tyler, president of the association, was one of the first arrivals at the new colony. He was followed by other members who came from all parts of the world to be saved in the faith and the association now numbers between five and six hundred persons.

Speaking of the association Brother Tyler said:

"We started in a rented house and we had faith we would succeed. With Mary and Benjamin as leaders, taking the scriptures as our guide we ever will succeed."

The first permanent building known as the House of David was built the same year. The building contained about thirty rooms, with a printing plant in the basement. Shortly afterwards becoming crowded for quarters another building of fifty rooms was constructed on Britain avenue, and shortly afterwards another house adjoining this of sixty rooms was built. Later a separate printing plant was built. Soon a power house, laundry building and work shops were added. About three years ago the zoological gardens were started, and now the gardens contain a vast collection of animals and birds, including wolves, foxes, bears, coons, etc and many rare birds from Australia.

Many of the members of the colony are expert agriculturists and the association has some of the finest farms in the township. Starting with five acres they have kept adding to their original until now they own several hundred acres.

About eighteen months ago the association commenced the construction of the first concrete and stone building and since then have added several. This when completed will be the office building and general headquarters.

Fire destroyed the frame printing plant also the power plant. Immediately plans were made for a fire proof printing, electric lights and power plant with a floor space of about three times larger than the one that burned. This was completed about a year ago.

The association raise more farm products than they consume. They have a large chicken farm with several thousand chickens, which they raise for laying purposes. The eggs they eat and sell.

The October freeze of two years ago damaged their peach orchards considerably. However, they immediately began replanting the orchards and also set out considerable small fruit.

While looking after their material welfare the association never neglects its spiritual advancement, and the members never fail to impress upon an inquirer the hope of immortal life.

News Palladium, Monday, July 20, 1908.

In 1910 Mary was given a golden watch by her husband, a watch that was made at the House of David's jewelry department. The inscription (right) was scrolled inside the cover with a burin by an unskilled hand; not at all matching the exquisite artwork and other lettering upon the watch done by a highly skilled engraver.

TO THE
ONE I LOVE
MARY
ALL THAT I HAVE
IS THINE
BENJAMIN

The House of David Blues
1927-1930

I set the children at war 3 years, that they may be separated, those that refuse to serve her, and I bound their writer at that time, hand and foot, as a sign to the whole house of Israel, that those that were numbered and still refused, that he should be a pattern for them. John Wroe, Vol. 2., page 869, Exeter, 25th of 9th month, 1833.

Your Honor,
I have one final witness
To call upon the stand:
The witness of truth.
And,
For the record,
The fact is:

In 1922 the legal counsel reviewed, and rewrote the laws of the Association, putting the power of the last word in the mouth of the Board and its Director, Mr. Dewhirst. Francis Thorpe would have to step down from his position held since 1905, as the colony's Secretary to become the Assistant to the Secretary, Mr. Dewhirst. Mary Purnell's name was no longer to be on financial receipts to the colony treasury. In the 1923 trial in Grand Rapids, the colony position was bungled when Mr. Dewhirst altered Attorney Sterling's outline of defense, and persuaded an ailing Benjamin Purnell not to come to Grand Rapids to testify on his own be-half. Mr. Dewhirst also successully lost the colony's appeal in the following year. With a Hansel victory the flood gates opened, as the Court awarded monies to the victors, which swelled the ranks of the little family conspiracy to defame Benjamin Purnell, break-up the Israelite House of David, and so divy up the wealth; the vision was now in accessible view. Had the colony been able to stop the Hansels in Grand Rapids, 1927 would have been just another average and normal year. So it was that in 1927, the location being changed to the Circuit Court in Saint Joseph, Michigan, the same characters would appear with help of the legal and political arm of that State in a civil suit, to pursue their desired death blow to Benjamin Purnell in particular, and the Israelite House of David et. al.

Over the years, and as many more came into the Israelite House of David, disciplines seemed to relax, rules were broken, and fabulous revenues accompanied with fame altered the fervency and integrity of more than a few. There were always the comers and goers; there were also the troublesome of habitual complaint; and as in all the world over there is jealousy and the politics of control and power.

The decade of the 1920's came to be one of trials, to sort it out: proving the men from the boys, as it were.

In 1921 H.T. Dewhirst would arrive at the House of David, which within months began the changes that would erupt into the court debacles, squabblings and open factionalism that polarized the Israelite home into 2 very determined groups. As the colony seemed to be in the court room most of the decade fighting detractors, defending it's founders, and finally, with a divided camp fighting for the right to exist without Big Brother's supervision; it seemed that the arrival of the former California Judge, His Honor, H.T. Dewhirst, would be just the God-send for the colony's legal ills.

What Mr. Dewhirst was able to accomplish in 5 short years, with his legal wisdom and prowess is still talked of to this day among the City of David folks, as to how quickly it all happened.

The following review is taken from "200 Years, Joanna Southcott-1792, through the City of David 1992." pages 43-52, R. James Taylor.

The John Hansel case heard in Grand Rapids, Michigan, in 1923 found a federal district judge waiving the legal written contract between Hansel and the House of David while he was a member at the community with his wife and family. In so doing, Hansel was able to sue and be awarded a monetary compensation for himself and family for the time he was a member of the association. This decision set aside the legal contract between the Israelite community and all of its associate members and ex-members. The defamation campaign against

Benjamin Purnell had been circulating since 1910 with the jealousy of Moses Clark, who left in bitterness, claiming Purnell had "debauched" his wife. The Hansels also used this surely demeaning scenario in the Grand Rapids trial, at which rumors of immorality were fanned into a great stink by the Detroit Free Press.

In 1923 the Bamford sisters, seeing visions of a plush reward, filed suits or "capias of rape" on Benjamin Purnell. These also were former members that had grown up at the colony and left with little kindness in regard to the Israelite way of life. Warrants for Benjamin's arrest were never served and later the suits were dropped, having no fact or foundation, and their attorney was finally disbarred for malpractice. Though the Bamford sisters failed, yet a conspiracy grew out of the Grand Rapids success, and the ring leaders were in fact the victors at Grand Rapids. This time the ranks of the plaintiffs had sizably grown, seeing monetary reward was available upon a proven complaint. Thus was launched the movement by a circle of conspirators, all former members of disappointed ambitions within the Israelite colony, and all related by marriage or blood. Rape and sexual harassment within the society leveled at the head man, Benjamin Purnell, had already proven success-ful in exciting the newspapers and creating an atmosphere of prejudice among the populace that, given enough headline time, would be difficult for any judge or jury to overturn with a fair evaluation based on fact. In the spring of 1927 the conspirators were able to enlist the Attorney General, with the grace of the Governor of the State of Michigan, to prepare a legal case to try Benjamin Purnell; and, if possible, bring an end to the reported public nuisance at Benton Harbor. Esther Hansel of Grand Rapids fame was funded by the State of Michigan to collect the plaintiffs together and coordinate a case that the local Berrien County legals were unable and unwill-ing to handle, in behalf of the people of the State of Michigan. The trial began as sensational national and international news coverage on May 16, 1927, and would become exhausted by August 17, in which 330 witnesses were called, 88 depositions taken, 500 exhibits were introduced, and 15,000 pages of testimony recorded. The State's Attorney-General had appointed a one-man grand jury: Louis H. Fead from Michigan's Upper Peninsula, to hear the case in which 13 young women gave their accounts of rape and sexual harassment upon themselves by Benjamin Purnell. During the trial, 221 of the 330 called voiced decidedly firm and opposite testaments in favor of Benjamin's innocence and upright character within the society for a quar-ter of a century. There were explicit descriptions of sexual misconduct as well as resolute defenses given on behalf of Benjamin. By 1927, in his 66th year, Benjamin Purnell was a frail and sick man of about half of his normal weight, suffering from advanced diabetes and diagnosed as having tuberculosis. His appearance in the courtroom was a pathetic instance of a legal infraction, if not a gross insensitivity to his failing condition. With a fever of 103 degrees and his inability to make his voice heard above a whisper, his attendant nurse from the colony, Sister Florence McCaslin, had to relate to the courtroom his replies to the interrogation. Benjamin's testament was innocence. The colony membership was a unanimous affirmative to his innocence. The very presence and continuation of the Israelite community is not in spite of his alleged guilt; no, but in the knowledge of his innocence.

During the course of the three-month-long trial, the entire workings and histo-

ry of the Israelite community was meticulously examined through both plaintiff and defendant witnesses. Daily life, tenets of faith, and procedural methods within the Israelite House of David were brought before the bench and public eye, and summarized in a bound 191-page review and "opinion of the court" by Judge Fead. The trial of Benjamin ended on August 17, which constituted the largest hearing in the county's history, with national and international coverage. Judge Fead retired to his home in Newberry to draft his decision which would be in waiting for almost three months. November 10, 1927, his "opinion" was filed with the Circuit Court which found Benjamin Purnell guilty of teaching and practicing perjury and that he was operating a fraudulent enterprise in the guise of religion. Judge Fead ordered an injunction to exile both Benjamin and Mary from the Israelite community, and to appoint a receiver of all colony assets to supervise the remaining membership, and to abate any further fraud upon the members of the colony or upon any new applicants for memberships into the community.

Contrary to the popular but incorrect assessment of Judge Fead's "opinion," Benjamin was not found guilty of rape, as the State of Michigan, on behalf of its citizens, was trying Purnell in a civil suit and not a criminal suit, under which rape or sexual harassment would rightly fall. The decree of the injunction was made public on December 5, 1927, calling for Benjamin and Mary's exile and the appointment of a receiver on behalf of the colony membership to govern its financial affairs. The decision of Judge Fead was immediately appealed to the State Supreme Court, and the exile was put on hold due to Benjamin's fragile condition. Much like Joanna's passing on December 27, 1814, was the passing of Benjamin Purnell 11 days following the decree for his banishment from the Israelite community, December 16, 1927. Both passed amid acute public scrutiny of both their person's and their life efforts as spiritual leaders to the Israelite people. Scorn, contempt, and derision followed both the "mother" of the latter-day visitation and its seventh messenger as they passed amid similar controversy and mystery, leaving the following believers with a trial for their faith, and the public with its prejudices seemingly fulfilled. In both cases the press was jubilant and unkind in its declaration of the demise of the Israelite messengers, with a decided mood of celebration at their passing.

"I will provoke the whole world by what I do unto that House (where thou dwellest); it shall be a sting to all that hear tell of it; and to all that is joined in my covenant, who are neither hot nor cold, it shall drive hundreds out of my flock; carriages shall stop at the place and shall hiss at it, and shake their heads; many shall look at it till they fall backwards into the ditch; not that it shall be a house different to any other house. And my people shall say, Ah!Ah! To see the falsehoods that there shall be in the papers concerning this house and thee, for thou shalt be tried for life and death; for all things that Israel has been guilty of from their mother's womb shall be laid against thee, and I will cause thee to bear it; whoredom, drunkenness, lying, murder, rape, witchcraft; this has been done since the days of Adam. So he that is my disciple shall mourn, weep, and lament and cry out against these abominations, and say, Ah! Ah! To see the great hatred of the adversary. (John Wroe, Private Word, Volume 1, 1825, p. 452.)

And 100s went out of the flock because of the public defamation and internal wranglings, that would thin the ranks from 1000 in 1916 to 435 in 1930. And the "yellow" journalism of the time speaks for itself, as to the many falsehoods that appeared in the newspapers.

"And I will choose seven virgins who shall live under one roof as in secret, till a conspiracy is brought against him, which will bring it into court. (Mary and Benjamin, Star of Bethlehem, 1903, p./ 520.)

Along with other exacting prophesies in the Star of Bethlehem, written 1895-1902, or 25 years before the event, as well as the recorded expectation of the coming legal and internal troubles, in meetings held at the colony from 1906 through 1909; those of daily life and faith within the House of David saw the 1927 trial as fulfillment of what they had been reading for a quarter of a century, and an event that must come to pass, that it be fulfilled.

As stated in the preceding, Benjamin Purnell was tried in a civil suit because it would yield upon conviction a monetary reward which was a chief aim, as Grand Rapids had yielded over $24,000.00 to the Hansel family.

"Prior to the trial, Esther Hansel interviewed certain witnesses for and on behalf of the State of Michigan, among them her brother-in-law and sisters, she stated to them as follows: "If you want to get money out of the House of David you want to put in your own claim now and be a witness for the state," and "All of the witnesses that testify for the state would get their share out of the colony property." It is an anomalous proceeding indeed that would permit the attorney-general as a relator to prosecute an action whereby the property may be decreed by the court to be confiscated and a receiver appointed because of fraud perpetrated upon the present members of the House of David, who have never made any complaint, and who are at the same time made parties defendant to the action. Also, "It is a peculiar circumstance to note that Benjamin and Mary (defrauders) as alleged and found by the "decree," are made co-defendants with the members of the association (the defrauded). And this not withstanding no present members have complained." And finally, "There is no law or authority for a court to exile a person in the State of Michigan." (Francis Thorpe, Crown of Thorns, 1929, p. 31.)

If the House of David were conducting a nuisance, as charged in this bill, there would have been 50 neighbors ready and willing to testify against the House of David. Yet no witnesses from Benton Township were sworn to substantiate the bill. It is a logical inference that not a single witness from Benton Township could be found to lift up his hand against the House of David. Therefore, in the spring of 1927, when it was manifest the state would have to dismiss the bill or look about for witnesses to substantiate the allegations of the bill already filed, Esther Hansel was delegated to make a fishing expedition in more than twelve states in the union, and the record in this case shows that of the 13 witnesses testifying against Benjamin, one was secured from the state of New York, another from the state of Washington, two from Indiana, two from Illinois, and one from New Jersey. And for this service on behalf of the citizens of Benton Township to abate a nuisance, the state of Michigan expended thousands of dollars in payment to these 13 witnesses." (Crown of Thorns, p. 21.)

No student of the Israelite history should be without The Crown of Thorns by colony assistant-secretary Francis Thorpe, which gives a deep insight into the conspiracy against the House of David and the judiciary blindness in the lower court's decision. Francis, with Mary Purnell and their faithful attorney William Barnard, formed the triumvirate to fight the appeal in the Supreme Court at Lansing. The authority of the decree began its motion, with the article of receivership put into effect, as the colony with attorney Barnard prepared their legal briefs in appeal to the State Supreme Court for a review of the finding by Louis Fead. The death of Benjamin eleven days after the decree issuance decidedly changed the circumstances of the injunction and Sister Mary remained at the colony unobstructed by any effort to instate her exile as required by Judge Fead. Because the death of Benjamin split the Israelite House of David into two camps, there were also two legal camps of appeal to the court at Lansing: H. T. Dewhirst, who led one colony faction had teamed up with attorney Foster, while William Barnard remained legal counsel to Sister Mary with Francis Thorpe and the other colony faction. The case before the justices of the state's highest court was of an entirely different aspect owing to the demise of Benjamin; and after long deliberation on June 3, 1929, the "opinion" of the court was issued from which the following are highlights of the 15-page brief.

This court having before it for determination a set of facts which because of the death of Benjamin Purnell is entirely different than submitted to the trial court.

Because of his death we find it unnecessary to review much of the record presented to the lower court or to determine whether the relief there granted was fully justified by the facts and circumstances as they then existed.

The whole case in its major aspects is centered about Benjamin.

This ruling does not, of course, take up the matters of religious doctrine for the purpose of determining the absolute truth or falsity thereof. It concerns only property rights, which are under control of the state, and neither prevents the members of the House of David from continuing, nor anyone else from commencing to accept Benjamin as the seventh messenger. Nor does it interfere with liberty of belief or the orderly and lawful expression of religious discipline and practice.

We know of no authority which would justify the state in attempting to intervene in a paternalistic way by means of a receivership work out collectively the various conflicting claims of the defendants. Especially is this true since the decree taken expressly provides that it does not contemplate the dissolution of the voluntary association.

The state had no right to institute this litigation for the purpose of securing an adjudication of issues in which it had no apparent interest, unless it can be justified in having done so on the theory that the incident to the abatement of the existing nuisance it was necessary to take possession at least temporarily of the property belonging to the defendants.

As the case is now presented to us, we must hold that the appointment of a receiver is not necessary to rendering effective to the decree of the court in abating the nuisance.

The decree entered in the circuit court is affirmed to the extent that the injunctive relief was granted incident to the abatement of the nuisance excepting that portion thereof whereby Mary Purnell is enjoined from going upon the premises of the association or participating in the management of its affairs as provided in paragraphs 2 and 4 of said decree. The other provisions of the decree must be vacated.

Signed by six justices, the "opinion" of the State Supreme Court was victory on the bottom line; and Sister Mary was free to maintain her standing position in the colony, which Attorney-General Brucker so much opposed in the state's brief to the Supreme Court, wanting instead the initial resolve of exile by Judge Fead to stand. The life force and living presence of Benjamin Purnell had organized, developed and commandeered the Israelite House of David to its worldwide renown, his death would leave an organization battered by a record of legal troubles, blackened by severely antagonistic journalism, divided in a bitter factional power struggle, thinned to a number of roughly 435 by late 1929. As severely as the authorities had probed the colony, yet the death of Brother Benjamin brought on the most bitter conflict of all, resulting in the division of 1930.

Fighting the House of David case in the circuit court in 1927—left to right: Attorney Foster, of the defense, the belligerent William J. Barnard of Paw Paw—now dead—H. T. Dewhirst—now King Ben's successor and legal counsel for his colony—and the then Deputy Attorney General Wilber N. Brucker, who was afterwards attorney general and later governor.

The first 10 years at the House of David were years of troubled health for Mary Purnell, it took long to heal from 6 years of a discomforting life on the road, and then aggravating that with the loss of her only daughter. The resiliance and fortitude of Sister Mary will from this time begin to show itself as circumstances will begin to draw her from without the shadow of her husband, and develop into the substantial figure that was, and indeed is one of the foremost ladies in the history of Berrien county.

In 1910 Mary would write Comforter #1 of the Mother's Book, followed in 1912 with The Comforter Book 2, which were listed in the catalogue of published literature available to the public from the House of David. Comforter #3 proved to be a controversial volume that her husband would recall, upon which ground Mr. Dewhirst would bar Mary from using the colony printing facility. Mary's 4th Comforter would remain in type written manuscript form from its completion in 1926, until the press of the re-organization would use it as its first publication in 1930.

By the arrival of the Dewhirst family in 1921, Benjamin Purnell's health had taken a decided turn for the worse, and the Judge recognized the opportunity that was given him to use. As the health of Brother Benjamin caused him to withdraw from the daily governing rounds, and as time went on, it became more difficult to see him personally; which surely played into the hands of the political mind in high places. The polarization developed during this period as the officers and managers were then given choice as to whom they would go for direction: Mary, the co-founder and spiritual co-leader; or Mr. Dewhirst, Secretary of the Board; who, by 1925, had galvanized a sizable number in support of his obvious entrepreneurial skills. Mr. Dewhirst was both convincing and impressive in the game of power and politics that he had so learned as an elected magistrate in the state of California.

A faithful woman can perhaps relate most sincerely with the trial that Mary Purnell would have to go through in the staunch and avid defense that she made for the man that she loved, bore children to, and had gone through such hardships with. Having bonded them into an invincible team that had outdistanced the jealousies that turned them and their young children out of doors in Detroit; that had started afresh after the Fostoria tragedy, leaving both parents solemn with grief; that would daily employ herself with all the concerns of the weak in faith within the home; that would stand up in the Courtroom to defend one whom she had been with through it all, and best knew the truth and innocence of her beloved. If it were not enough that she be tormented with the harassment from an unkind and decidedly bias Press against her husband, and in the midst of all the ridicule and embarrassment, once again she would feel the crushing blow to a mother, as she outlived both her beautifully-petite, little Hettie; and now her son of 43 years was dead. Samuel Coy passed on 27 January 1924. With a husband of digressing health; a pending court trial, which included embarrassing charges of immorality and fraud addressed to him; a home once glowing with the vibrance of Christian love, and now bitterly being divided over power and wealth; and her very position of authority being brought into question by a growing faction within her home of 20 odd years. And on top of it all, the death of her only son. Amid these despairing and hurt-

WORLD'S FAMOUS
HOUSE OF DAVID
SYNCOPEP SERENADERS
DANCE - CASINO - FRAMINGHAM
FRIDAY EVENING, APRIL 24
UNDER THE MANAGEMENT OF GRACE DEARTH FARNSWORTH

Seldom, if ever again, will we be able to present a banner feature of this calibre. We urge you and your friends not to miss this extraordinary event.

These longhaired, bewhiskered Kings of Syncopation are beyond question the most unique and biggest attraction in show history. Meet them at The Casino, Friday evening, April 24.

The Shaveless Sheiks of Syncopation Played to 12,231 Paid Admissions at Cleveland Public Auditorium, Friday Evening, February 13th.

BE SURE TO SEE THEM!   **BE SURE TO HEAR THEM!**

ADMISSION: GENTLEMEN, 75c: including Tax: LADIES, 50c: BALCONY, 50c

Every Arrangement Has Been Made to Handle a Monster Crowd

Of all the Israelite talents that Benjamin Purnell would help develop, the two travelling jazz bands of the 1920s were the premium product of them all. They were major league from their beginning under the tutelage of the Hannaford family patriarch, Joseph Hannaford, being part of the 85 Christian Israelites from Melbourne, Australia.

ful trials did Sister Mary Purnell, at age 62, begin to show forth the buds of the ever blossoming vine, continuing to thrive in the beauty of unquenchable faith and unconditional love, that truly and unmistakeably is of the Christ. It can only be genuine, and recognizably true, when it is the joyous survivor of the trail of tears, the stench of humiliation, and the other cheek offered to the back hand of cruel rejection from within your very home. From the years of 1924-25 unto the re-organization of 1930 would Sister Mary begin to blossom into the mother figure that would lead a faithful and resolute remnant from their comfortable homes, and by court order, into the chilling March winds, and yet another new beginning.

The Hannaford family from Melbourne, Australia (1905) were all music. They built instruments, taught music and played them all with the guidance of the family patriarch, Joseph Hannaford. With the many young families that came to the House of David, there was a pool of talents waiting to be encouraged, and all were given opportunity to play an

BASEBALL! **BASEBALL!**
at EAST N. Y. OVAL
ROCKAWAY AND CHURCH AVENUES
SAT'Y, JULY 22, 3.30 P. M.
THE MOST TALKED OF EVENT IN BASEBALL CIRCLES
HOUSE OF DAVID BEARDED GIANTS
FROM BENTON HARBOR, MICHIGAN
— VS —
EAST NEW YORK A. A.

The House of David Team is the Biggest and Most Unique Attraction in Baseball
Don't fail to see this World's Famous Religous Collection of Baseball Stars
Every arragement has been completed to handle the enormous crowd

COME EARLY   GATES OPEN AT 12.30   **BRING THE LADIES AND CHILDREN**

Directions: Wilson, Ralph-Rockaway, Church Ave., Bergen St. changing to Wilson Ave. car direct to Park. Interborough Subway, Pennsylvannia Ave. Train get off at Rockaway Ave. B'way Canarsie 'L' get off at New Lots Rd.

GET WISE — OWL PRINT, 384 Central Avenue, 387

instrument or to sing in one of the many musical and voice ensembles in the colony. The House of David jazz band, The Syncopep Serenaders, were the blue chip performers of the Israelite community. They were all big leaguers, with the Hannaford family forming the foundation of the two travelling bands that played with the best of them across the American continent.

Benjamin Purnell loved baseball, and by 1913 there was a team assembled with colony Secretary, Francis Thorpe as its manager. Through its colourful history into the early 1950s, the House of David, and later City of David teams would produce some major league performers, and delight all of America with the featured "pepper game." In major league exhibition games the Israelite ball club would beat the boys from St. Louis, and Connie Mack's Philadelphia Athletics. In one particular exhibition match with the New York Yankees, the House of David pitcher, Percy Walker would strike out the "Babe," and Ruth would give Walker his bat.

Re-printed from "News Palladium" Nov. 26, 1926

GIVE 'KING' BEN CHANCE, PLEA OF CHASE OSBORN

FORMER GOVERNOR COMES TO BAT IN DEFENCE OF COLONY LEADER

DETROIT, Nov. 26—Benjamin Purnell, "King" of the House of David, is not the ravisher of young womanhood he is painted as being, and care should be exercised in assuming too readily that he is guilty of all the charges against him, former Governor Chase S. Osborn declared today.

Osborn, when governor, investigated complaints concerning the Israelite colony, and made a personal inspection of the place less than two years ago.

"NEVER SOLD A GIRL"

" 'King' Ben has never sold a young girl," he said. "Mrs. Vanderbilt recently admitted she sold her daughter in marriage to an Englishman. Purnell has not done things the 400 in New York have done or that people in Hollywood do every day."

"Benjamin Purnell should be given a square deal. He has lived in Michigan many years. The people of Michigan should not accept too readily some of the things being said on the assumption that he is guilty."

No "HARD LOOKERS"

"Women's faces betray them. When I visited the House of David I saw no hard-faced women. I saw women whose faces betrayed simplicity and innocence. There may have been some who appeared cowlike, or stupid, but I saw none who looked hard."

"I do not believe 'King' Ben to be guilty. If he is, the place for him is an asylum, not a prison."

"We don't know what the motives of some of 'King' Ben's accusers might be. Women sometimes will make complaints because they have been balked in efforts to shake someone down."

"There are many factors in the case which make it far from a certainty that 'King' Ben is guilty."

"KING" BENJAMIN, ET AL

Editor, News-Palladium:

I am very favorably impressed with your public enterprise in throwing open your columns for public discussion.

Not being an attorney, I may be mistaken but it has seemed to me that a state's attorney was supposed to prosecute, not persecute, and it does appear that all this furore over the House of David smacks somewhat of persecution. Neither do I think that it is exactly dignified to indulge a predelection for bombastics by rushing into public print in highly vituperative and denunciatory terms. I assume that, as usual, this case will be tried in the courts and not in newspapers. I simply cannot find myself flying into spasms of virtuous indignation because a few women of doubtful mentality wish to flaunt their shame in public for the sake of a pecuniary reward. I hold no brief for Benjamin; if he is guilty he should be punished the same as any other malefactor, but let us at least reserve judgment until his seeming guilt becomes a fact and not an assumption.

I call attention to the fact that no other member of the House of David has ever been brought into court on a criminal charge and that is something which cannot be said of any other community in our county of equal population. In fact I have always found the men of the colony to be courteous, kindly, helpful if needed, industrious to a remarkable degree and with a mentality above rather than below the average, I do not grant them or any other group the right to dictate my religious beliefs but neither do I assume the right to dictate to them.

Outside of this one accusation—which is yet an assumption merely and not a proved fact—can anyone point to one thing which these people have done which violated any statute or sense of public decency? But almost anyone who is acquainted with them can point to not only one but very many things which have served to aid the community in general and the public at large.

It has been said that an empty cask makes the greatest sound. Now of course that saying could not possibly apply to our present prosecutor, but it might be made to apply in some degree if these howls, growls, moans and groans of righteous indignation are not conserved to a greater degree.

May I not humbly suggest that it is a mistake to waste ammunition shooting at shadows even though it may be highly diverting to the public.

With the kindest regards for all involved, I am, yours truly,

L. BENJ. REBER.

STATE OF MICHIGAN

IN THE

CIRCUIT COURT

IN AND FOR THE COUNTY OF BERRIEN,
IN CHANCERY

———

PEOPLE OF THE
STATE OF MICHIGAN, ex rel.
ANDREW B. DOUGHERTY,
Attorney General,

Plaintiff,

vs.

ISRAELITE HOUSE OF DAVID,
A Voluntary Association, et al.

Defendants.

No. 5167

———

ANSWER OF DEFENDANTS

Now come all the defendants herein by W. J. Barnard, their attorney, and for answer to the amended bill of complaint, and the amendment thereto, respectfully show unto this Court:

FIRST

The defendants admit that Andrew B. Dougherty was the duly constituted, qualified and acting Attorney General in and for the State of Michigan at the time of the filing of the amended bill herein, but deny the existence of any facts, or the commission of any acts which authorize the interference and the interposition of a bill in equity at the instance of the Attorney General.

SECOND

The defendants deny that they or any of them have been guilty of illegal or wrongful acts in the form or manner complained of in said bill of complaint, or acts which tend to the public detriment and affect or endanger the public safety and convenience of the People of the State of Michigan, or any acts which require any judicial interposition in this behalf.

THIRD

The defendants admit that the property interests involved in said suit are of the value of more than one hundred dollars.

FOURTH

The defendants deny that the Israelite House of David is now, or was at any time, organized for fraudulent, unlawful or immoral purposes, and deny that any immoral practices have inhered in said organization by or with the connivance or consent of any of the officers of said association, or at all.

Defendants deny that there is now, or ever has been, a combined or concerted action on the part of said officers, or the members of said association, for the perpetration of any fraud upon its members, or the public, or the commission of any unlawful or immoral acts and practices.

The defendants allege in this connection that their bylaws and Articles of Faith have been publicly proclaimed since their adoption in December, 1907, or for a period of nearly twenty years continuously last past—and in addition thereto said bylaws have been recorded of record, both in the office of the Register of Deeds and the office of the County Clerk in and for the County of Berrien, State of Michigan, and also in the office of the Secretary of State in and for the State of Michigan; and that by reason thereof, there is not now, and has not at any time been, any legal excuse or reason why either the public officials or the general public should be, or profess to be, in ignorance of the faith and teaching of the House of David.

The defendants further allege in this connection that the bylaws and articles of faith as so recorded, and the user thereunder, conform in all respects to the teaching of the Holy Scriptures, and furthermore, the exercise thereof is in accordance with the rights of religious tolerance and freedom as vouchsafed by the provisions of both the constitution of the State of Michigan, and of the United States.

The defendants deny that their bylaws, or their religion, is in any manner borrowed or used fraudulently as a cloak of religion to disguise their true purpose or motive; and they further deny that the same is used for the purpose of enriching Benjamin, the Head of said colony, or for his private gain; and they deny that he has been at any time using the same as a cloak for the gratification of lust, or the commission of any criminal or licentious practice.

The defendants admit that Benjamin Purnell has been from the time of said organization of the House of David, its Head, and as such has directed the affairs of said association in accordance with the provisions of the bylaws thereof, and not otherwise.

FIFTH

The defendants admit that there was organized in 1903 a religious corporation known as the Israelite House of David, the Church of the New Eve, the Body of Christ, but they deny that the same was in any manner organized for the purpose of defrauding the rights of its members, or the People of the State of Michigan.

Five of the twenty-one articles in the opening statement of William Barnard, attorney for the House of David, 1927.

"You might think I hate to leave this house which has been my home for so many years. The house which Benjamin and I fought and worked so many years to build. That is not so. The only reason I ever fought for this property which belonged to me and my followers, was because they had worked a life-time and I felt it was their right to have it. But now I know that I am to come into my own. I know now that success is with us and we shall grow, and grow beyond our wildest expectations.

"All the outside trouble of the colony in the last few years was as nothing compared to the internal strife in our midst. For peace is the very foundation of our belief.

"I agreed to the settlement because I am through fighting," the new leader declared. "Our faith is based on peace. Our very doctrine is based on that one great theory. I want peace for myself and my followers. We shall get along some way. I must make a home for 217 of my followers somewhere within the next few weeks.

"If our fruit crop is good on the farm, then all will be well. We have until April 1st before we must all be gone from here and the Jerusalem headquarters. We can live in tents, in log cabins, any place. We shall be free. We have kept our Faith. God will see that our fruit trees bloom and bear for us. We shall triumph through it all."

"I have faced hunger and thirst here in Shiloh fighting for my very life. But I won through. My followers consider all this a victory for us. We go out with their sanction. We have some farm lands, and the town building. There is canned fruit on our farms, and vegetables. We shall build a new headquarters here in front of the little yellow house which must serve for a while.

"The only clothes I've had are what kind friends have sent me; this dress, these shoes, these stockings, are all gifts. For the folks in power, led by Dewhirst, would give me nothing."

Mary has no fear, she feels no anger. She has only regrets and commiseration for H. T. Dewhirst, the lawyer and judge who came from San Bernadino, California, ten years ago, and with whom Mary has battled to the end for control of the Israelite colony since Benjamin 'went away more than two years ago.'

"This is the end, for them" and she smiled and shook her head. "Me and my followers, we have lost only our money. We have agreed to go, taking little with us. But we take our faith. The others who remain within the old House of David have lost their faith. They have broken the covenant. We have only pity for them."

It was during the long legal battle that the State of Michigan waged against the House of David, trying to dissolve it because of a conspiracy against Benjamin" by disgruntled women members who wanted money, that Sister Mary bore the brunt of the battle against her and Benjamin.

Sister Mary said, "At the last not only did I have to fight the State, but H. T. Dewhirst in his capacity as one of the attorneys for the House of David who turned against me and tried in every conceivable way to oust me from the colony. He and his followers put every indignity they could think of to bear upon me and my followers, and as Dewhirst had control of the money, the books, and the board, they denied us the necessities of life, in food and clothing, and every false and hateful innuendo against me and my people were circulated among the members and the public as well. Advertisements were placed warning the merchants not to sell to me or to members of the board who represented me. These are recorded facts in court, and as published by Mr. Barnard, our attorney, from time to time, and in reviewing the many published items we find this one of much interest, published in the News-Palladium, October 3d, 1928:

From Mary's Story of the Separation.

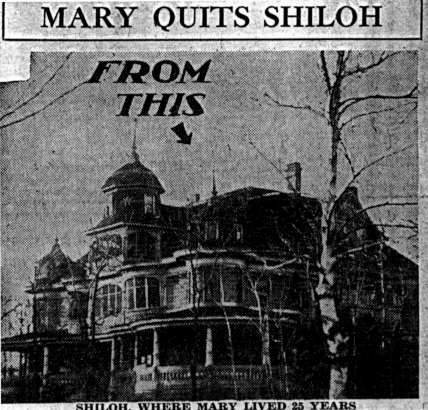

FROM THIS ↓

SHILOH, WHERE MARY LIVED 25 YEARS
"Queen" Mary Purnell and her late husband, "King" Ben, ruled the House of David from this building in Benton Harbor. Under Mary's agreement with H. T. Dewhirst, house and her rule pass.

TO THIS ↓

—Photo by Times Staff Photographer.
MARY'S NEW "SHILOH"
This frame cottage in Benton Harbor is the headquarters for the reorganized House of David over which Mary rules. More than 200 faithful followers left the colony with their Queen.

With the death of Benjamin Purnell there came an end to the subtleties between the already strained and distant feelings between the Dewhirst faction, and those loyal to Mary. When it became evident that peaceful co-existence was not a possibility, Mary went about to do what a spiteful family and two Michigan Court decisions failed to do: dissolve the Israelite House of David. And then start a reorganization with those that would remain faithful with her, unconditionally. The singular prize was peace; and then a place to call home after a long day's toil. Just a place to continue the sim-

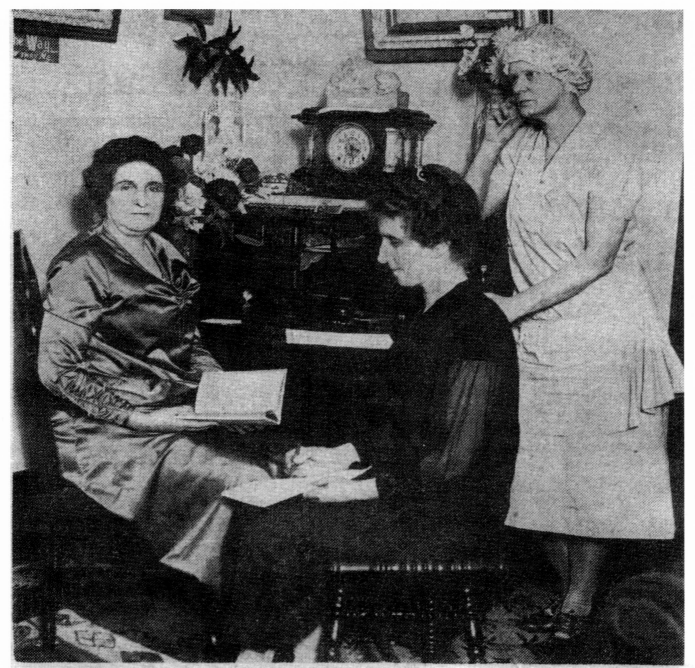

"QUEEN" MARY

Leading her flock out into the world again, Mary has rallied her loyal followers around a new "Shiloh." She's shown with her faithful secretary,

MRS. EMMA ROWE

Mrs. Rowe, examining the book Mary turned out on a typewriter because Dewhirst wouldn't let her use the House of David presses.

MRS. LAURA CONNAN

Mary's house would be headquarters of the Re-organization from April 1, until just before Christmas of 1930.

ple practice of daily faith these 217 now proved was all they desired along with her. The separation had achieved something that only such dire circumstances could bring about: the workings of Christian brotherhood as all else around them had failed. The early days of the reorganization is the most moving chapter of the second hundred years (1892-1992), and the one that truly witnessed the workings of the Israelite faith against all odds over the entire 200 years. Mary Purnell at age 69 was now the Ensign to the Israelite people, and was the rallying figure around which the 217 would build a new city, and families would continue to come in from the far reaches of the earth. Mary had come into full blossom as the inspiration to her people, INDEED THE VERY EXAMPLE OF WHAT SHE TAUGHT. Not since their first coming to Benton Harbor in 1903, even back to the hysteria in England over Joanna Southcott's final days, was there such an excitement in the camps of Israel.

With the Bakery already in operation at 563 Eastman Avenue (left), and the tent still standing across from Mary's house at 540 Eastman, Mary and Francis Thorpe stand to the foreground (left of center) at the excavation site for her new Auditorium building in August of 1931.

A new beginning. With such veteran names in her ranks of longstanding faithfulness are Silas and Cora Mooney that were in the original seven from Fostoria; George, Frank, Otis, William, Theodore, and Archie of the Baushke family that first gave the House of David property and monies to make a beginning in 1903; Francis Thorpe, the faithful first Secretary from 1905; Christov Krishart, the builder of many of the fine buildings on the Eden Springs property; Bob Vieritz, the agricultural captain of the host; and many other names of great importance to the survival and provi-

dence for the remnant: Louis Manthey, Homer Baker, Mabel and Estelle Hornbeck, the Tucker family with four young healthy men, etc.

Just two blocks east of where they came to build in 1903, some of the very same would begin to build again. And for the third time in her sojourn, with the breaking of spring, Mary Purnell would leave a home's comfort for a new and uncertain beginning, with conviction for what is right, and faith in God; that there IS providence for the ever faithful.

Although Mary was co-founder of the House of David, and the faith taught from 1 Corinthians, chapter 11, the man is not without the woman, neither the woman without the man, in the Lord. (verses 11-12), which in fact set the Seventh apart from all the former Six Messengers, yet she would remain as one among many within the community. As in the photograph above, in looking closely you will see her in white, with a ladies hat, 7th in from the left.

Once the hour came for her to arise to the occasion, she would indeed prove to the faithful remnant of 217 that she was equal to her husband's leadership; and in giving her 4th, 5th, and 6th books of The Comforter to those in fellowship, she would be no less than convincing that the dove of the Spiritual graft from the 12th of March, 1895, in Detroit, Michigan, would follow the ever faithful in truth into the building of the City of David.

The large and new tent purchased by the Re-organization would serve as a Meeting place, and also a storage for the many trunks and belongings until new homes could be built by the end of 1931.

In 1912 Mary Purnell went to the photographer's studio at the House of David to make the picture to be placed in her second book of The Comforter, published 12 March 1912. As the camera man took aim, one of her doves came to light upon her head, and the click of the finger gave the colony supporters of Mary the symbol of her divine authority, as rightful heir to the leadership of the Israelite House of David, upon the death of her husband in December of 1927.

Crown of Thorns

S

HOUSE OF DAVID

VICTORY

and

LEGAL TROUBLES

REVIEWED

S

Internal Strife
Cause and Effect

S

By FRANCIS THORPE
Assistant Sec'y., House of David
Benton Harbor, Michigan, U.S.A.
P. O. Box 175

Cover of the Crown of Thorns, 1929, authored by Francis Thorpe, then assistant-Secretary for the colony. In late 1904, while Mary and Benjamin were away on their world tour via Melbourne, Australia, Francis would come to the House of David from Marshalltown, Iowa. He would be made first Secretary for the colony in 1905, but would step down to H. T. Dewhirst in 1921. He would be one of Mary's most outspoken supporters and defendants, forming the triumvirate with her and attorney William "Wild Bill" Barnard to win an appeal to the State Supreme Court in June of 1929; and would be Mary's right hand in the Re-organization, and the early financial success of the City of David.

Francis Marion Thorpe, 1905, handsome and charismatic, he would serve the Israelite community for 53 years as one of its most visible leaders; one of the original 5 male Pillars of the City of David, and one of the 3 co-Trustees with Mary in 1952.

Francis didn't wear a glove nor swing a bat, but he knew talent when he saw it. He would advertise, get connections, and then take the best squad of young Israelite players out of Benton Harbor to dazzle audiences across America, and become a legend in their own time.

House of David Base Ball Team

Francis Thorpe,
1929.

QUEEN MARY IN HARD BATTLE
DEFENDS SELF AND KING IN APPEAL CASE
STANDS BY BENJAMIN

Still Insists State Witnesses Reviled the Colony
Founder.

"The brief embraces 117 printed pages and re-
cites in great detail why Judge Fead's decree, from
which Mary is appealing, should not go into effect.
If the Supreme Court sustains Judge Fead's decree
it would mean the break-up of the House of David
as well as the exile of Mary from the colony grounds.

Benjamin's exoneration of Mary is quoted in
the brief. Said Benjamin on the witness stand from
his stretcher:

**"Never, never did I suspect anything carnal con-
cerning Mary."**

The Brief shows that 52 "female witnesses" were
called by the State against the colony, and parts of
the testimony of many of these witnesses are quoted
to the Court in which Mary was exonerated from
any alleged misconduct.

"This mountain of testimony" says the brief,
"cannot be brushed aside by mere innuendoes or base
insinuations. For days, weeks and months she was
dragged through the filth and mire of this trial and
emerged therefrom without a stain upon her character. With all the barrage of vilification and cal-
umny directed at the House of David this defendant
came forth unscathed and unharmed."

Barnard's brief paints Mary as a queenly
woman of rare traits of character.

"With all the malice, venom and bitterness exhibited by the State's witnesses" says the brief,
"they were without exception forced to admit that
this defendant was kindly disposed toward all, that
she bore her burdens gracefully, was charitable and
forgiving. This is illustrated in the testimony of
Gladys Blankenship and Ruth Swanson. She had a
well defined idea of infinite forgiveness, a lifelong
yearning tenderness, a nature sublime, with a
sympathy that went out to the old, the feeble and the
sick; her chart was love, patience and kindness. She
did not believe in governing by force, threat or any
other form of coercion. It was not her nature to
arouse in the hearts of God's creatures a thought of
fear, discord, hate or revenge. It was her aim to
influence people by aiding them, uplifting and ad-
monishing them with teachings from the divine
Scriptures to which she had devoted more than 25
years of her life. The Faith she taught and advocat-
ed was the life she lived for a period of more than
30 years. She had the courage of her convictions
and the Record fails to show that she desecrated
that ideal by word, thought or deed, and Benjamin bore witness to this when he said: 'Never—
never did I suspect anything carnal concerning
Mary.' "

Brother Francis Thorpe would also take up pen and ink, after the Crown of Thorns, and write The Mantle of Shiloh, 1946, and The Royal Seed, 1947, which were published at the City of David and included on the available publications listings. Below is his outline of the Israelite faith included in the Crown of Thorns.

ISRAEL'S FAITH SIMPLIFIED

The following is written with a view to simplify:

Israel's faith being so broad, new ones are troubled about getting a clear grasp of this faith. Here are some of the questions often asked by others:

In what way does your faith differ from other churches?

We teach eternal life on this planet, of body, soul and spirit; all, or nearly all other sects or churches teach death on this planet, of body and a spiritual mansion in the skies afterwards.

Who is head of your church?

Christ is head of the church, and He is the Saviour of the body. Eph. 3-23.

Do not all sects claim the same?

No, they do not. Many claim Christ to be the head of the church, but deny he is a saviour of the body.

Is there anything written of such as deny this saving power?

Yes. Many passages: Paul says, They have a form of Godliness, but deny the power thereof.

Do you believe in a Resurrection of the natural body?

No. The scriptures only show a resurrection of the spiritual body if you die; a body once dead goes to corruption, turns to dust, and is eternally damned. Job says, He that goeth down to the grave, shall come up no more. Job. 7-9.

Then you think all will be lost if they die?

No, certainly not. Their natural body is lost, but all will be saved or rewarded with a spiritual body according to their faith.

You think then, some will have a greater blessing than others, and that all will not be just alike?

It makes no difference what anyone thinks, we go by what the scriptures say. Jesus said, In my father's house are many mansions; and Paul says, There is one glory of the sun, another glory of the moon, and another glory of the stars; for as one star differeth from another in glory, so also is the resurrection of the dead.

Then according to that, some would have a natural, immortal body, and others only a spiritual body of resurrected soul in Heaven.

Can you give further proof of these two classes or three classes?

Yes. Jesus referred to two classes when he said, I am the resurrection and the life, he being the resurrection for the dead, and the life for the living. Paul says, There are bodies celestial, and bodies terrestrial, and the glory of the celestial is one, and the glory of the terrestrial is another. The terrestrial means body of flesh and bone, the celestial being a spiritual body. He is coming to judge the quick and the dead. The quick are the living, who are found alive and will remain. It was Simeon that held Jesus a babe in His arms and said, He shall be a light to lighten the Gentiles, and the glory of His people Israel. Luke 2-32. He has ever been a light to the Gentiles, but now he is come in spirit to be the glory of His people Israel, the living.

Why did not Jesus show the distinction when he was teaching?

He did when he said, I am not sent but unto the Lost Sheep of the House of Israel, but as to the soul salvation he said, Go ye into the world, and preach the gospel to every creature. Mark 16-15.

Yes, it would be very absurd to expect life and follow nature, for man by nature is carnal, and at enmity against God —is not subject to the will of God, neither indeed can be. Rom. 8-7. And if we live after the flesh, we shall die; and if we sow to the flesh, we shall of the flesh reap corruption; but if we through the spirit do mortify the deeds of the body, or suppose we sow to the spirit, then the scriptures say we shall live. As in Adam all die, even so in Christ shall all be made alive, but every man in his own order. Then get in Christ and live.

Why is it that this life of the body teaching has not been taught universally?

Because the time had not come. The time is near when the knowledge of God shall cover the earth as the waters cover the sea, but now darkness covers the earth, and gross darkness the hearts and minds of the people. Men are prone to unbelief, as Jesus said, though one rose from the dead, ye will not believe.

What will cause people to believe this?

They will be quickened by the spirit, and believe what the prophets have said.

Is this a new religion?

No, it was taught by Enoch over four thousand years ago.

Did he not receive it?

Yes, he is a living witness of life. By faith Enoch was translated, and saw not death. Heb. 11-5.

What things are necessary to do in order to become a true Israelite?

Get a good understanding of the life of the body from the scripture, by seeking to the spirit, and studying the word; give up all pride, and lust, or anything that savors of evil. You will then be in a position to love God and keep his commands. This do, and thou shalt live.

What did Jesus mean when he said, Greater love hath no man than this, that he lay down his life for his friends?

It is written of Jesus, that he died that we might live. He is the only true friend of man that we ever had to visit us on this planet. Many sects sing of how they love Jesus, but where are the people that are willing to give up all for him? Jesus being our friend, if we lay down our life of evil for Him, it is a proof of his word being fulfilled in us, and proves that no greater love hath any man than this. Israel will have this love, and will overcome as He, Jesus, overcame, and their reward will be Immortality—swallowed up of life.

'The Echo Of My Mother's Voice'

Written by Mary of the House of David

Just After the Trial Was Finished. September 29, 1927

The echo of my Mother's Voice. Oh, Mother, Mother! who is like unto Thee? I can only wonder and wonder how it is that woman rises at the very front when any great advance is made. Was this not shown forth in the case of the Virgin Mary; for did not God, the Father, overshadow her by the power of the Holy Ghost, and did she not conceive and bring forth His First-born Son, Jesus? There is a savory sweetness to this grief of a broken hearted Mother. Did she not follow His steps to the cross, and is it not written that she followed Him from the judgment hall to Calvary's hill? Can you not see Him moving along slowly, and almost ready to drop down under the thorny crown beneath the cross; and the Blessed Virgin Mary, still a woman, still a mother, almost ready to faint by the way?

Oh! we can imagine her hiding her eyes from the scorners; and pushed aside by those who knew her not; and those who did know her hated her for her goodness and purity, but still through the help of the Almighty God she bore up on her sad journey through the Valley of Humiliation, and how bravely she withstood the brutality when those cruel hands drove the cankered nails through His darling hands and feet of the One she loved so dear.

Oh! the thoughts of that terrible hour of suffering have ofttimes brought tears to many an eye, and he who understands to any degree a mother's heart it is easy to believe that she was absent when the cruel mob raised that Holy One upon His cross.

Sorrow penetrates the language of love to its deepest depths, and when the end was approaching Mary and John stood side by side near the one who to them was dearer than all. It was a woman who bore Him through all the persecutions and frowns of an unbelieving world before this Noble One bore His cross; and reverently I say it, Woman's cross is ever set and all the earth is her Calvary. But must not she suffer all these things and enter in... ...you must think, that all of this pain ...bring a victorious blessing for the rise of fallen man; to bring him back to that estate from whence he fell.

Let it be remembered whenever you discern a prophetic character, emblem of Christ, forerunner of the golden age, you will find for his partner and help a woman; for the manhood of Jesus reflected the sweetness of His Mother, the Virgin Mary. And the true soldiers of the Lord Jesus Christ will honor this Queen of Women, Our Lady, a Woman girdled with the Virtues of her duties, being endowed with the golden sceptre next to Christ, God's best gift to man, "For a virtuous woman is a crown to her husband," and I am here today to proclaim her rights, and in doing so I shall appeal to those sure words which survives when all else fails; she proving herself to be of the royal lineage of the House of David; the noble One of all the earth because the seed of Jesus being within his loins;

for did not Jesus say, "I am the Root and offspring of David, the bright and the Morning Star:" The Root being Christ and the offspring being the seed that was within David's loins, the bright and Morning Star because there was no evil within Him.

Let it be remembered it is the Mother who impregnates the life which is in the heart of the child; therefore when men holds this virtuous woman to his heart he has that precious gift of all the earth, and they both receive the choice things of Heaven; for did not God give to woman, and not to man, to co-operate with Him in bringing our Saviour into the world?

So let all give praise unto this Virtuous Woman, which is Jerusalem, Above, (Gal. 4-26) showing forth our faith what every woman should be, and he that deals nobly with the one by his side will find her bringing in a glory that will establish God's Kingdom of Peace here on earth.

Therefore, let us remember Joseph who was such a beautiful figure of Jesus in is brief and suffering, being sold by his own brethren, put his ear to mother earth and found comfort and consolation in the echo of His Mother's Voice, saying, "My Son, My Son, Joseph! I have heard the voice of thy weeping, and the voice of thy tears, I know thy trouble. Therefore, My Son, Joseph, My Son! Hope to the Lord and wait for Him, for the Lord is with Thee, He will deliver Thee from all trouble."

Therefore, let us ever remember that noble One Jesus whose heel (heal) satanic man bruised upon the cross, which signified taking away His healing power from off the earth, and as His heel was bruised upon the cross so now at this the time of His second coming through the power of that One Immortal Spirit will the head of satan be bruised, which signifies his power will be taken from him.

Therefore this calls my mind back to Joseph, the espoused husband of Mary, who was found worthy to be entrusted with the virgin for well did the God of Heaven know that he would harken to the Voice of that Angel whom he sent with the command to keep her a virgin. So all Israel will be content when they feel and know they have the approval of God in their conscience, of which their hearts greatly yearn for the approval of that One man Jesus Christ who was once here upon earth; whom we dearly love, who now sends His good angels from His very throne to watch over His people Israel as they drift about in strange places, cared for by the God of Heaven as Ishmael and Elijah for whom He prepared water for the one and bread for the other; and the same God sent the Holy Family, viz, Joseph, Mary and the Babe to Egypt with the charge to stay there until He brought them word. So now let us understand whomsoever God sends in His work He charges Himself with their supplies, and no doubt Joseph, Mary and the Babe found many Israelites in Egypt who

had sought refuge from the persecutions round about their own homes. Doubtless these exiles received Joseph, Mary and the Babe with gladness of heart, and we cannot help thinking of this Noble Woman who follows the footsteps of the Divine Christ.

The enemy may think to do us wrong, but by the presence of the Divine Mother Jerusalem Mother Above their hearts fail them, and instead of them fighting against us they are willing to fight for us, and protect us in every way they can, proving God holds the key to every heart.

And now sweet it is to meet with one of these outcasts suffering for Christ's sake, fully realizing the crown of thorns we must wear, and from the crown of thorns comes forth the beautiful Rose; yea, the Rose of Sharon. And it is then we shall hear the Father's Voice saying, "Welcome home, ye wandering pilgrims."

This is indeed a trying hour but my loyalty to this Most Holy Faith never grows old or cold, but always unto me as a beautiful garment. Therefore let us ever keep constantly in our hearts the wonderful words of the Arch-Angel Gabriel, and follow on strictly in the footsteps of the Firstborn Son, Jesus, who was a destroyer of death and a Saviour of life. As we behold this Noble One who went forth to heal and to preach let us ever encourage His beautiful words within our heart; yes, with praise and joy, for the Dove of Peace from Heaven rested upon Him at the River Jordan; but how soon did He disappear thus entering into the wilderness, it being the time of His temptation; and after 40 days we behold Him returning to gladden their hearts, but how soon did the enemy set forth the new trial and this Noble One was driven out from His own people, but His faithful Mother never wavered in Her loyalty to Her Son, and indeed this act on her part not only revived the hope and faith of the disciples but renewed the zeal of her motherhood which strengthened her in the most trying hour. She was willing to stand all things to win for Her Beloved, and the black clouds gathered blacker and blacker around; she being despised and rejected by those who claimed to be in the faith; thus hating her without a cause; and I never will forget these trying days, but a ray of hope comes within my heart as I fully realize it only helps me on my way to the New Jerusalem, the City of God. Yes, longing and longing to walk the same narrow path of which our Master trod, for my heart's desire is to be in company with God's people, not to be looked upon as a beautiful creature to be admired, but there to pray with those who pray for the fulfillment of the Word of God, and although I walk slowly on we are drawing near and nearer and our journey will soon be complete. I know He, the Lord, will not fail me.

And we behold all the world longing for some golden day better than the present, for He said, "I will come again;" then Mother and Son will again fill the earth with all their glory, and all the nations shall call them Blessed, because of the Father, Mother and Son, for by them this Mighty Work was done. The figure three all linked in one.

From the News Palladium, September 29, 1927, Sister Mary's answer to the trial's controversy, as in all of her life's trials, was her complete trust in God who provides for the ever faithful.

1930
The New Beginning

**A design by Benjamin Purnell that was used on page 7
of the New Shiloh Messenger since 1930**

Aerial photograph from 1937; in seven years, while the nation was only modestly recovering from its economic colapse of 1929, most of the City of David was built. The name "City of David" for reasons of brevity, and to distinguish themselves from the Dewhirst colony, became the legal title for its business enterprises on December 14, 1933.

'QUEEN' MARY STARTS ANEW WITH FLOCK

Reorganized Cult Accomplishes Wonders In Two Busy Years

The House of David, as reorganized by Mary Purnell, in two years' time has built a new city unto itself.

Under the leadership of "Sister Mary," widow of the late Benjamin Purnell, founder of the religious cult, the new colony now boasts 10 major buildings.

Only little more than two years ago, when the final split between her faction and the Dewhirst adherents came, Mrs. Purnell started anew with one small dwelling, a three-car garage, and a large tent.

Today the 12-acre plat of ground on Britain avenue, east of the old colony grounds, is dotted with a large new administration building, shops, a new restaurant, auditorium, bakery, lumber mill, canning plant, chicken house, and the start of a new park.

Build Tourist Cabins

In addition five log tourists cabins have been constructed, and four more will be added during the coming year.

The colony at the same time is growing in membership. When the split came 260 of the faithful followed Sister Mary from the old colony grounds. Today the membership is nearly 300. New families have come from Australia.

At the present time two more families are on their way from New Zealand.

And over all presides "Queen" Mary, with a new smile of confidence and happiness.

"It's all so very wonderful. It never could have been accomplished without the co-operation from every member," she declared.

A Self-Contained City

The reorganized Houes of David, like the one organized by Benjamin 30 years ago, is truly a city in itself. There is a printing shop, carpenter shop, auto repair shop, blacksmith and tin shop, a central heating plant for the shops, a water system and sanitary system, a modern bakeshop, a canning plant, a harness shop, electric shop, saw mill, shoe repair shop, a public restaurant, and a public park and playground, along with an auditorium where the religious services inaugurated by Benjamin are still conducted by Sister Mary.

The heating plants are modern, with automatic stokers An oil burner is used for cooking in the main kitchen of the administration building.

Many of the buildings have living quarters for the members on the second floor. A small green house has been started.

The administration building is the last word in modern construction, three stories high, with an exterior of brick.

In addition to the "City of David" as the members call it, the colony operates approximately 700 acres of farm land which more than supplies the members with foodstuffs.

The chicken house on the colony grounds is populated by 500 white Leghorns.

Owns Hotel Building

In down town Benton Harbor, the colony also operates its hotel building at Elm and Colfax, with stores on the lower floor, where clothing, fruits and vegetables, and baked goods are sold, and another public restaurant operated.

The colony already has its summer supply of ice cut and in the ice house. Advantage was taken of the pre-winter cold snap two weeks ago to flood lowlands where Blue Creek joins the Paw Paw river, and 300 tons of ice was harvested.

MARY ORGANIZES A NEW COLONY

Following the death of "King" Benjamin Purnell and years of bitter litigation, The House of David split in twain. "Queen" Mary, breaking with H. T. Dewhirst, led a group of loyal followers to a new colony east of the original one. Her flock is known as the Israelite House of David, reorganized by Mary Purnell. It is now a thriving community, growing steadily. Above are some of Mary's colonists, hard at work on new buildings.

Reorganized Members April 1st 1930.

Mary Purnell.	Joseph Brugger	Wm. Fredericksou	Frieda Jones.
Cora Mooney.	Wm. H. Bewley	David Foust.	Lois Jones.
Silas Mooney.	Iola Boykin.	Wm. Groves.	Chrishart Krishart
Francis Thobpe	Daniel Boykin.	Alvina Grimm	Frank W. Keller
Emma Rowe	Georgia Curtis	John R. Gardner	Amelia Klynn
Jane Kipper	Richard Callahan	John E. Gordon	Goldie Link
Arthur Abbe	Joseph Couch	Thomas A. Gray	William Link
Lizzie Abbe	Elizabeth Couch	Reinhold Holm	Theo Lepp
Ila Abbe	Job. Couch	A. G. Hayes	May Lyman
Julia R. Anderson	W. B. Caudle	Nels Hansen	Robert Lyman
May Anderson	Jettie Caudle	Guy Hendrickson	Frieda Lange
George Anderson	Bernice Dee Caudle	Roy Hendrickson	Davilla A Myers
Jas. L. Austin	Charles Crowe	Margaret Hendrick	Jennie Martin
Gustav Alexanderson	Nannie "	Joshua Haynes.	Wm. H. Martin
Margaret Abell	Miles "		Wilma Martin
	Sudie "		

Frank Baushke	Jimmie Crow	Conrad Hartman	John Martz
Theodore Baushke	Henry Caudler	Mollie Hartman	Nedra Martz Abbott
Ohio Baushke	Wm. H. Connon	Kate Holliday.	Albert Monier
Winnie Baushke	Laura Connon	Emily Hill	Mary Monier
George Baushke	Molina Charter.	Roland Hill	Louis Mauthey
Max Blume	Cora Darst.	Estel Hornbeck	Daniel Murphy
Jos. A. Browning	John Degman	Martha Holman	Isabel Miller
Julius L Baker	Mary D'erbam	Sallie Haynes	John Mottram
Walter Boruff	Gideon Drew	Jesse Haynes	Angelina Mottram
Emma C Boruff	Lionel Averett	Elversie Haynes	Michael Meany.
Raymond Boruff	A. A. Estry	Daisy Haynes	B. O. Moe.
Wilce Buck	Herman Erickson	James A. Hanson	Peter Mahoney.
Lewis Buck	Mattie Edmunds	Harley Harrington	Agnes Nelson.
Everett Buck	Amos Edmunds.	Fred Hoffman	Elisha Nelson.
Wm. H. Buck	Andrew Euton	Albert Hedrick	Ramon Nelson,
Lewis Buck Jr.	Joseph Averett	Martha James.	Mary Ellen Nelson,
Lou Buck	Veda Averett	Ashley Johnson	Otto Nelson,
Lee Buck	Claudia Flake	Sarah Johnson	Luther Nelson
Albertine Baushke	Pearl Flake	Evan Johnston	Bammie Nelson
	Wm. H. Frye		George Neilson

Margaret Nelson
Exd Mae Nelson
George Nunley
Wm. H. Nigh
Albert Ogden
Augusta Paton
Wm. H. Phillips
Paul Perrenoud
Peter Post
Lou M. Petitfils
Sarah Rogers
Ada Rubel
Addie Rubel
Jacob Rubel
Tony Rubel
Etta Reed

Henry H. Snow
Leonard Shumbler
Peter Smith
Mary Smiley
Lucy Tappenden
Frank Tappenden
Ella Taylor
Emma Tucker
Chas. J. Tucker
John R. Tucker
Uber A. Tucker
Melvin A. Tucker
Cecil Tucker
Walter Trotter
Elizabeth Truckimiles

Edith Tally
Jesse Lee Tally
Duncan Tart
Ella Tart
Henry Tart
Henry Troupe
John Van Dalen
Bob Vieritz
Mary   "
Norma   "
Chas. Vieritz
Mary J   "
Doris   "
Clive   "
Mary Vaughn
Julius Wilson
W. R. Wiltbank
Francis Wort

Monroe Wulff
Elma
James Winder
Eth. Winterbottam
Ethel Walker
Charlie Walker
Mary Warner
Sadie Warner
Christina Walter
B J. Wilkison
LaVinia Walker
Ernest Walker
Chas. Springs

Leslie Reed
Atta Rains
Mary F. Reed
E. R. Reed
Pearl M. Rein
Wm. H. Rein
Edith Rein
Ida Robertson
General Robertson
Mary E. Ross
Edward Reinert
Louis Reinhardt
Virgil D. Smith
Gertrude Smith
Samuel Sipes
Ross Smiley
Axel Sydow
George Smith

All the above Members were the original 217 who
came over with Sister Mary from the Old House of David.

'Queen' Mary Builds
New House Of David
Near Old Home

Huge Construction Program Includes Six Large Bldgs.

Headquarters On Britain Avenue Expected To Be Completed By October; Contains All Modern Conveniences

A "new" House of David is in the making just a block east of the old colony grounds.

"Queen" Mary Purnell and members of the Reorganized House of David, as the group terms itself since the split with Judge H. T. Dewhirst, are in the midst of a huge building program.

One building is completed, four others are in the process of construction, while the foundation is in for the sixth. More buildings are planned for the immediate future.

Build New Headquarters

The largest building now under construction will be the new administration building. It is 70 by 40 feet, with three full floors, although a complete basement with extra high ceiling, and dormers on the top of the third floor make it practically a five story structure.

It is being constructed of small hollow tile, resembling red face brick.

A block east and south another three story building, constructed of concrete block and frame, is rapidly moving toward completion. It will be used primarily as living quarters for the members, although one end will be fitted up into a printing shop.

Erect Shops

Directly across the street, workmen are finishing up a large two-story building of similar structure. The lower floor will be used as work shops, the upper as sleeping quarters.

The concrete foundation is in for an auditorium to be 70 by 50 feet, with a 500 seating capacity. Here "Sister" Mary intends to hold religious meetings this winter. At the present time, meetings are held in a large tent.

Another three-story building nearly completed will be used as a laundry on the lower floor, with sleeping rooms above. This is another masonry and frame structure.

The building already completed is the bakery. It is built of concrete blocks, and equipped with a huge modern oven in which 300 loaves of bread may be baked at one time, a large mixer, and other modern baking equipment. For the present the front of the bakery is being used as a general dining room.

Queen Mary Happy

"Queen" Mary is superbly happy. The joy of creation simply bubbles out all over her.

"When the settlement was made," she explained referring to the property split between her followers and Dewhirst's adherents, "our people were without homes. They had to leave headquarters and find places as best they could.

"My first thought was to provide rooms for them. It's just like starting all over again, just the way it was back in 1903." The colony was first founded here in 1903.

"The bakery was built first. They had kept us without bread for months, you know, and our first step was to provide a place to do our baking."

Pulling Together

"Now we are wonderfully happy. Everyone is pulling together, and I think we are making big strides. Everyone has been so kind to us. Load after load of building materials have been given us which has come in pretty handy.

"This place is truly the new home of Israel."

Sister Mary's new administration building looks like a hotel. Equipped with every modern convenience, it is somewhat different than the first buildings constructed when the late Benjamin Purnell came here in 1903 and founded the religious colony known as the House of David.

It has electric lights, modern bathrooms, heated by an oil furnace. It has sun parlors and cozy fire places.

The bed rooms are large and well lighted.

Across the front is a large double decked porch, 14 feet by 50 feet.

It opens into a large reception room across the front. Mary's private office is directly to the east,

with a fire place, and a sun parlor. This floor also contains the offices, and several bedrooms to the rear.

Contains Mary's Apartments

On the second floor are her apartments, with another reception room opening on the upper deck of the porch, a living room, sun parlor. Here, too, is another fire place. This floor contains eight bedrooms.

The third floor contains nine bed rooms, and the fourth, formed by dormers, provide sufficient space for several more.

Each floor has a modern bathroom.

The basement, well lighted by reason of its high ceilings, contains two dining rooms, a kitchen, fruit rooms, the heating plant, a Williams Oil-O-Matic furnace, and a large wash room.

There is another sun porch along the rear of the building, underneath of which is a general work room.

It is hoped to have the building completed by October 1.

Lacking land on which to build, Mary acquired 11½ acres, east of the old headquarters property on the south side of Britain, by trading lots owned in Benton Harbor.

A wooded ravine is being made into a park. It is named Paradise park.

Sister Mary hopes to have the auditorium completed by winter that she may abandon the big tent which for a time served as sleeping quarters, meeting house, and storage place, even during the last heavy snow fall. The basement will be used as a laundry.

For the present she continues to live in the modest little home built as the intended exile home for herself and Benjamin following Judge Fead's decision, banishing them from the colony. A stay was granted by the state supreme court, but Benjamin died before the court finally reversed Judge Fead's decision in the state receivership suit against the colony.

A second floor was added to the garage to provide sleeping quarters.

Sister Mary announced that many new members have entered her Reorganized House of David.

More than 10,000 letters have been written to prospective members answering inquiries concerning the faith, according to her secretary, Laura Connon.

The contractor in charge of the construction of the new headquarters is a new member of the colony.

Mary eagerly is waiting the completion of the printing shop that she may print her new book she has completed embracing the House of David faith. Seven copies have been finished and bound in book form, with the pages numbering 539, all typewritten.

As soon as the present building projects are completed, she intends to start the construction of several log cabins along Britain avenue.

ISRAELITE HOUSE of DAVID
FURNISHED ROOMS

Clean, Cool and Comfortable
With Bath

Good Meals Served
At All Hours
Prices Reasonable

MARY'S HOUSE

**Eastman Avenue, Third Street East of Headquarters,
Second House South of Britain Avenue,
Benton Harbor, Mich.**

In the early summer of 1929, Mabel Hornbeck would open up Mary's house for rooms and a small restaurant in the basement. The venture was one for the sorely needed income that Mary Purnell would need upon the soon expected settlement with the Dewhirst faction.

In front of "Mary's house", Sister Mary is center-right, holding her hat; Estelle and his wife Mable Hornbeck are first and second from the left, 1930. Following the Decree of the trial Court Judge, Louis Fead, in December of 1927, the Israelites faithful to Mary, purchased the vacant lot at 540 Eastman Avenue and laid plans for the building of a residence for Mary and Benjamin, if the State's highest Court would not relieve the injunction for the Purnell's exile from the House of David colony property. Called Mary's house from its days as a blueprint, Mary would move into the 2 story, full basement home, and make it her headquarters until her new Shiloh building would be ready, in the rough, by Christmas of 1930. Mary's house has now served as a residence for the City of David membership for 66 years; in 1994 and 1995 the entire exterior surface was renovated.

PEACE

PSALM 133

Behold, how good and how pleasant it is for brethren to dwell together in unity.

It is like the precious ointment upon the head, that ran down upon the beard, even Aaron's beard; that went down to the skirts of his garments;

As the dew of Hermon, and as the dew that descended upon the mountains of Zion; for there the Lord commanded the blessing, even LIFE FOR EVERMORE.

Honour to Whom Honour is Due

Cora Mooney would become Mary Purnell's closest associate in their 52 years together, beginning in Fostoria, Ohio, in 1902. Known for her outspoken and staunch defense of both Benjamin and Mary in a life long faithfulness at the Israelite community as Mary's chief aide of the immediate household. Cora was one of the original female Pillars of the House of David, and later would be one of the City of David's original 5 female Pillars. She served faithfully 61 years until her death in 1964.

Of the most faithful in fellowship with Benjamin and Mary, from their home in Fostoria, Ohio; and through the thick and the thin, are the persons of Silas and his wife, Cora Mooney. They with their son, Paul, were three of the seven that arrived in Benton Harbor 27 years earlier to establish the home base for the Seventh Church, 1903. Silas was sincere, longsuffering, faithful, and a hardworker with the Israelite farms from the beginning. One of the original 4 Pillars of the House of David, he would also serve as one of the original 5 male pillars for the City of David, and was one of the co-Trustees with Mary in 1952, and until his death in 1957. Silas Mooney was the very definition of consistent dependability for his Brothers and Sisters, serving with immovable faith in his community for 54 years. The earliest of Mary's entrusted lieutenants, Silas wore work boots, bib-overalls, an old felt brim hat and five stars within his heart.

Robert Vieritz, born in Queensland, Australia in the year that Benjamin and Mary first heard the "Extracts From the Flying Roll", 1888. With his wife, Mary, who was 3 days younger than her husband, and daughter, Norma, Bob would bring his little family to the House of David during the high-tide years of the first World War. Their entrance into America was not an easy passage by reason of a German name, and of foreign birth. By the mid 1920s, Bob Vieritz would rise up in the agricultural part of the Israelite community, and come to oversee the largest farm of 655 acres, the Rocky farm, which became a crucial stake for Mary in the settlement with the Dewhirst group in 1930. Kindly disposed, handsome,

and a model of strength and long hours; Bob became one of Sister Mary's lieutenants, and a name of respect in Berrien County agriculture. Along side of the management of the Rocky farm, a community within itself, Bob would serve as a Pillar and later a co-Trustee until his death in 1961. It was the numbers of genuinely good people in fellowship with Mary Purnell that made it go and prosper; it was the numerous gentle, hardworking and industrious folks, of whom the name, Bob Vieritz, was one of her best. Bob would oversee one of the county's largest farms, and the show piece of Israelite agriculture for over 30 years.

Mabel Craig and Estelle Hornbeck, would meet and later marry in the Israelite House of David. Mabel, from Forth Worth, Texas, (her father would send away for plans, scale down, and build the miniature steam locomotives for the Eden Springs Park in 1908) was a seamstress, cook and manager that would quickly come into her own during the Re-organization. She would open and manage the restaurant and boarding at Mary's house until the vegetarian restaurant, for the summer resort, would open on July 3, 1932; which she would manage for 30 years. From an accident in her youth, Mabel was stone deaf; but could read lips, even lips hidden by Israelite beards. Once upon meeting a delivery man at the restaurant, who was chewing on a cigar, she asked him to take the cigar out of his mouth so that she could understand what he said. He did so. And they continued on with their conversation and the ordering; he, never knowing that she couldn't hear a word that he said. The cigar was blocking the lip movements which she was able to read and understand.

Estelle Hornbeck's family from Springfield, Missouri, were the very first family called to Benton Harbor, in April of 1903. Estelle would learn to play the trombone and make one of the travelling jazz bands, touring in the early 1920's. One evening, around 1912, Estelle would accompany Benjamin Purnell for an evening, after supper walk, eastward along Britain Avenue. At about a block from the House of David property, Benjamin would stop and point to a gentle rise on the south side of the street, where there was standing an apple orchard; he said to Estelle, "Estelle, I believe I am going to build a house right there on that spot." Estelle asked him, "Do you think that I will live in it, Brother Benjamin?" Benjamin replied, "Yes, I believe you will." 18 years later Estelle Hornbeck would help build the new Shiloh headquarters building on that spot, and live there until his death in 1982. Along with almost 75 years of service to his community from 1903, Estelle would serve as a pillar to the church from 1954-1982.

Alice and Eunice Bond arrived from Christchurch, New Zealand on the third day, of the third month, in the thirty-third year, at 3:00 in the afternoon; being two of three sisters that would come to the City of David. Their father was an English immigrant from London, a follower of James Jezreel, who would in turn accept Mary and Benjamin as the Seventh Messenger before he died at Christchurch, and three of his seven children would embark for America.

Sister Alice Bond, right, would become the meticulous bookkeeper for the City of David, and later for Trustees, Francis Thorpe and Bob Griggs, keep community financial information at their fingertips. Alice Bond would be seen in many places throughout the colony as one among the many willing volunteers where ever extra hands were needed to make the work load a little lighter; she would also serve as a Pillar of the church until her death in 1970.

Sister Eunice was a professional seamstress by trade, and upon coming to the City of David was soon to be personally appointed by Mary Purnell as one of the original 5 female Pillars. She, with Brother Baker, would manage the summer resort office, and later would manage the apartment office of Mary's Apartments, while serving as a Trustee; the only female in that capacity other than Mary to date. For 25 years Sister Eunice would edit the monthly New Shiloh Messenger, and correspond with the many subscriptions abroad, keeping her post as editor and Trustee until her death in 1992.

One of the finest examples of Christian-Israel was the soft-spoken, mild-mannered, Eunice Bond. Whose day would begin at 5:00 a.m. with little feet patterings down the Shiloh staircases to her office, to which she would turn the lights out at 10:00 p.m.—seven days a week for 48 years of devoted, patient, and loving service. Amen.

Louis Manthey, picture above, left, came from Queensland, Australia, with a party of 10 in 1918; among those in that group were cousins, George Anderson, and May Anderson, who would also stand with Mary Purnell. George would become the famous athlete in the City of David's baseball and basketball teams for over 20 years, while his sister May would help manage yet another successful Israelite enterprise, the City of David Greenhouse.

In 1935, Louis Manthey would step down as co-ordinating manager of all the fruit crops for the colony, and would begin to build and operate the greenhouse from that year until his retirement in 1976. Manthey was another one of multi-talents: he would oversee the restaurant addition in February, 1937, giving it now twice the area; he also cut the stones for the foundations and entrances, above grade, for the 5

log cabins, 1930 and 1931. The greenhouse was a great success under Louie's management and green thumb, and for 41 years the rich and the modest all met, in the spring, at the City of David Greenhouse. The well-to-do, because Louie had the finest flowers and vegetable plants around; the more modest of means, because the prices were also the most reasonable in the area. How could he do that? Well, there are no labour costs to be figured into the retail or wholesale price when the operation is both managed and worked by a commonwealth brotherhood. Louie Manthey kept prices low and quality high for 41 years, he would also serve as a Trustee from 1954 until the year of his death in 1978. Louie Manthey was another one of the many wonderful personalities that knew long hours, 7 days a week; in dependable sincerity to the fellowship with Mary Purnell.

The court order for Mary and her people to vacate the House of David by April 1, 1930, was far reaching, in as much as James Taylor, his wife Laura, and their son Freddie, would also have to pack and leave their home (since 1919) at North Ryde, Sydney, Australia. With their clothing, personal items, and his carpentry tools, the Taylor family would stay with Sydney area relations for 2 years, while James would find carpenter work daily (during the Depression); and finally would build a summer home for the Worth family of England (International Worth Circus) which enabled them to afford passage to America in May and June of 1932, upon Mary Purnell's request that they come home. Bob Griggs, who had arrived just a month previous with his family from Oklahoma, came downstairs in Shiloh to hear beautiful singing out on the porch, on the morning after the Taylor family's arrival. He went out to see who it was, and met Brother Jimmie; Bob said that he saw the happiest man he had ever seen in his life, that morning. Being a carpenter by trade, and familiar with the reading of blueprints, James Taylor was soon at work, and would work with the carpenters at the City of David for over 25 years. Building doors, windows, trusses for most of the new construction at the colony, he would oversee the Studio building addition in 1942, design the Court building in 1939, design and build the buildings at 1335 East Britain Avenue in 1948. He also would be instrumental in the building projects of the Synagogue, King David Hospital and the Carpenter shop at the City of David.

The picture taken at Blue Hole, Lane Cove Road, Sydney, Australia in the early 1920s, is a telling photograph. James Taylor, to the far left, was one of two parties at Sydney that would stand with Mary Purnell; and the Taylor family was the only family to be called by Mary to come home from Australia. The rest, as pictured above, would remain in the Dewhirst camp, keeping their homes; homes that Brother Jimmie helped design and build.

Brother Homer Baker was from Pennsylvania, and of a Quaker background. He would be the designer, and manager in building many of the City of David buildings. Brother Baker was in charge of building all of the resort cottages from 1932 through 1939; the Jewish Synagogoue of 1938, and the re-modelling of the Eastman Springs buildings in 1945 were also under his supervision. During the summer months Homer was in charge of the resort office, and would serve the Israelite colony as a Trustee from 1956 until his death in 1962. Brother Baker was known for his soft-spoken manner, and a gentleman. Another fine example of Christian Israel, and the calibre of people that built their own community, as Berrien County watched the "beehive" of activity in a time of little money, scarcity of work, belt tightening, and sacrifices the world over.

Following with Mary Purnell into the Re-organization were three of the greatest names in House of David baseball, keeping the "pepper game" alive with the three stars of it.

George Anderson, left, came as a boy with the Manthey-Walker-Anderson group from Australia in 1918, and would excel in David Harrison's junior teams of the late 1920's. Anderson would bring excellence to the already famous "pepper game", being able to roll a baseball across his shoulders and the back of his neck, from elbow to elbow. Later he would also star in the City of David's travelling basketball team, which would use the antics of the baseball "pep-pergame," bringing it onto center court. The act quickly developed into another sensation using tricks, and showmanship with the larger ball. The basketball act was caught onto by some of their opponents in the black teams, ran away with international fame known as the Harlem Globetrotters.

John Tucker, center, came with his family from Tyler, Texas in 1915. While the family went up to the High Island lumber camp, it was a few short years later that John was back in Benton Harbor at home plate, with a baseball bat in his hands. An old black gentleman told me years ago, how he would play ball against the House of David teams (or "Jesus' boys," as the Kansas City Monarchs called them), and he spotted Tucker as a skinny-spindley youth with a world of talent. He told me that, "He and Brother Benjamin were the first to know that John Tucker was a ball player." John Tucker became the Israelite team showman, and perhaps their greatest athlete; both in his long Texas-stretch, from his position at first base, as well as his consistency at hitting baseballs. Through their many exhibition games with the Kansas City Monarchs, Tucker became a life long friend of the legendary, Satchel Paige, who is still pitching for the Cooperstown organization. Clare Adkin, author of Brother Benjamin, 1990, petitioned Cooperstown for the admission of John Tucker into America's Baseball Hall of Fame. The petition remains unanswered due to insufficient records of the Israelite Baseball Club over the 20 years that John played baseball there.

Jesse Lee Talley, right, born at Red Oak, Oklahoma, would come with his family to the House of David in the early years just preceding baseball at the colony. Jesse Lee "Doc" Talley would be one of the very early stars of the 1913 prize squad that

Francis Thorpe would take on the road that year, in the beginning of a legend that would draw crowds throughout America, and shut down entire towns on a Saturday afternoon for almost 35 years. Of the many bearded stars that would step up to home plate, and send the outfielders looking for he ball, "Doc was the Babe Ruth of the ball club, being one of the originators of the "pepper game", and later he would play with the Israelite travelling basketball team. Talley would make athletics his career as he

played the game for all the 35 years in an Israelite uniform, almost to the year of his early death at age 53, in January of 1950.

Uber and Melvin Tucker, 2 of 3 brothers to John, spent 12 years on the High Island lumber camp (1915-1927) growing into the young men that would help muscle the Re-organization into a productive and self-sustained community. High Island was a fond, and often recollected memory for the Tuckers; a pioneer upbringing on an island in upper Lake Michigan,

without electricity or running water. But they had the time of their lives in building their own skis and toboggans, hunting wild blueberries with the native American Indians on the island with them, and swimming in the crystal clear waters of Lake Michigan that surrounded them. Once they would climb a towering white pine to steal an eagle chick, and then raise the bird to maturity, after which they would set it free. Often the bald eagle would return to circle the camp, and upon occasion, if one of the

Melvin Tucker (left).

Uber Tucker (right).

boys would raise his hand into the air, the eagle would swoop down to light upon his shoulder. I'd say a fair exchange for having to cut your own fuel to burn through the long winter months.

High Island would not only supply lumber to the House of David until 1927 for building and sale, but would also grow enough potatoes and other vegetables, on the new cleared land, to feed themselves and send quantities home to Benton Harbor. On new cleared land, in a short growing season, the vegetables were both large and sweet. It was for this purpose that the House of David purchased and manned great lakes cargo vessels, to transport both lumber and vegetable produce from the newly cleared forest lands of High Island. The House of David had purchased 5000 acres of the island in 1912, with the docking facility, and a lumber mill that had gone out of business. This island property would be awarded to the Dewhirst faction in 1930, and would remain abandoned from 1929 until its final re-sale to the State of Michigan in 1957. The Tucker family came home in 1927 along with most of the lumber community; no lumbering, no produce after 1927; for the work force would come home and join in with Mary Purnell and by mid-summer of 1930, the Rocky farm was providing trees for the newly built lumber mill to saw into lumber for the City in its building.

Uber Tucker was another one of many talents in both carpentry and cabinet making; but his finest work was in his vegetable gardens. Handling a variety of produce over several acres, Uber would have one of the most productive and beautiful vegetable gardens in the area. Uber Tucker would also help build a house that never existed. While spending 12 years on the island, he would help in the construction of a summer log cabin residence for summer vacationing parties from the Benton Harbor headquarters, which was later fictionalized as the "harem shack." For the final record, and from the mouth of one of the many who were there, Benjamin Purnell visited High Island one time at its purchase in 1912, before the colony refurbished the sawmill and began building the log cabin communi-

ty, that would grow to the number of 150 lumbermen, sailors, cooks, farmers, teamsters, carpenters, and the many children with their families.

Melvin Tucker, third of the four Tucker boys, became the utility man of the family, for the numerous jobs that he would fill over a period of 72 years. From the Rocky farm fruit packing shed, to raising corn and soy beans on three different farms, working in the summer resort restaurant, driving the baseball team as its manager, to truck farming. Today Melvin is 88, and has been a member of the colony for 81 years; he has been both a Pillar and a Trustee for 35 years. With many fond memories of High Island, and the enthusiasm for the Re-Organization, Melvin told me that he went to Sister Mary with a complaint about the "favored" young people, while at the old House of David colony. It seems that certain ones got preferential treatment, and could break the rules that other boys got called on to the "carpet" for; such as frequenting the ice-cream parlor, and apparently sporting their obvious privileges. Sister Mary's comforting reply came from the bigger picture, "Brother, did you ever stop to think, that this is all that they are going to get?"

Another time she would tell Melvin in a conversation, "To be ready to give up all but your faith." For faith is the substance of things hoped for, the evidence of things not seen. So the Tucker family, with Mary would exchange the ice cream parlor, and their beautiful homes for peace and the keeping of their faith; and with little more than faith, began building the evidence of a faith proven by works.

Left to right:
Bill Totten, Daniel Askerlund, Harry Snow, Bob Griggs, Annie Griggs, Daisy Lambert, Malvola Parnell, Emily Monier, Adeline Vaughn, James Sutton, Martin Snyder.

In June of 1932, Robert D. Griggs, his wife Annie, and daughter Marie, would arrive from Shawnee, Oklahoma, and add to the growing list of newcomers to the City of David. Bob was of executive material, and completely a southern gentleman, who quickly was given the managing position at Mary's Hotel in downtown Benton Harbor; replacing Brother Baker, who was needed back at headquarters to begin the construction of more summer resort cottages along Britain Avenue. Bob would immediately begin an intensive advertising campaign for rooms, the hotel cafe, the bakery goods shop, and floor space on the first floor for area businesses. Soon with a little re-structuring, along with the ads, Bob was able to fill the 90 rooms, rent business spaces to fill the entire first floor available, and the vegetarian cafe would become a popular breakfast and lunch with the downtown business loop. This new and rapid income is what Mary needed to keep the wheels of progress moving ahead. Coming at a time so needed, Bob Griggs would prove himself faithful in fellowship with the Israelite community, and a man of steel. Bob would work his 12 hour shift at the hotel lobby desk, 7 days a week, from June, 1932, through March, 1975, (42 years and 9 months). There was Lou Gehrig, and maybe Cal Ripken, but really, there was Bob Griggs. Along with his 12 hour a day duties at Mary's Hotel, in 1956, Bob would replace an ailing Francis Thorpe, as the colony Secretary of the Trustees, and would keep the community steady through a difficult period of the 1950's, whose conservative means and wise investments continued the well-being of the City of David for 25 years. Bob would resign as a Trustee in 1978, due to his health, but continue serving as a Pillar for his people until his death in 1987. He and his wife, Annie, are among the many fine, gentle, and industrious folks that came to the commonwealth of Israel, in fellowship with Mary Purnell.

Jerusalem Above is Free,
The Mother of Us All.
Gal. 4:26.

Another Comforter, Whom
The World Cannot Receive.
John 14:16-17.

THE NEW SHILOH MESSENGER

THE STAR OF BETHLEHEM

Mothers ✶ Book.

In those Days and at that time, will I cause the Branch of Righteousness to grow up unto David:
And He shall execute Judgement and Righteousness in the Land. In those days shall Judah be
saved. And Jerusalem shall dwell safely and this is the Name wherewith SHE shall be called.
"THE LORD OUR RIGHTEOUSNESS."
Jer. 33: 15-16.

Behold, I bring you good Tidings of great Comfort and Joy

VOLUME 12

And it shall come to pass in that day, that the Lord shall set His hand the second time to recover the remnant of His people. Isa. 11:11.
For a small moment have I forsaken thee, but with great mercies shall I gather thee. Isa. 54:7.

NUMBER 8

MISSION OF CHRIST'S SECOND COMING

Christ's First Coming Was for the Soul By the
Atonement. His Second Coming Is for the
Bodies of His Elect—He Being the Shepherd
of Israel, Head of the Church and
Saviour of the Body.
Rom. 5:11; Jer. 31:10; Eph. 5:23.

I AM NOT SENT BUT UNTO THE LOST SHEEP OF THE HOUSE OF ISRAEL. MAT. 15:24.

By Benjamin and Mary

The Spirit of Truth which Jesus promised to send is now come to gently lead and guide His people in the way of all truth and show us things to come. The Son of man shall send His Angels, and they shall gather together His Elect. John 14:16, 17, 26; 16:7, 8, 13; Matt. 24:31.

Thousands today, look for Christ's coming, but do they understand the time and manner in which he comes? This is the most important thing—to be ready. But we can only just briefly bring a few scripture statements to bear upon this great subject, for two reasons: First, because time would fail us at present, and secondly, because many things pertaining to these unspeakable words are not lawful to be uttered in the outer court. 2 Cor. 12:4. The Spirit of truth which was to be sent, and has now come must gently lead his people in the way of all truth as they are able to receive it; yet they are to be led in the way of all truth and shown things to come, but not all at once—it must be step by step up into the temple of wisdom. Prov. 4:7.

The Son of Man to Send His Angels to Gather Together His Elect. Matt. 24:31.

Jesus said: I am not sent but unto the lost sheep of the house of Israel (Matt. 15:24); but while the sheep are scattered over the mountains of Christendom, we must say: I have many things to say but you cannot bear them now. However, it is written: When the Son of man shall come, the

Shepherd of Israel, the sheep shall be gathered from among the nations, and he shall keep them as a shepherd keepeth his flock (Jer. 31:10); and unto Shiloh shall the gathering of the people be (Gen. 49:10); and he shall send his angels to gather them from the uttermost parts of the earth and heaven, etc., and by the law of separation they shall now be separated as a shepherd divideth his sheep from the goats. Matt. 25:32. Therefore this time of separation has come, and he is calling his sheep out from among them that they might be separated; and he says: Touch not the unclean thing, and I will receive you, and you shall be my people, and I will be your God. I will make a new covenant with the house of Israel after those days—i. e., after the fulness of the Gentiles be come in (Rom. 11:25); which time has come, and the messenger of the covenant has come (Mal. 3:1), and I will write my laws in their inward parts and stamp them upon their minds; and this is the sealing in the forehead. And there was sealed 144,000, which shall be the manifestation of the sons of God. Rom. 8:19.

HARK TO THE CALL

Hark! Jah—Jehovah loudly calls,
Come, prostrate now before him fall,
Lest you too late should feel the rod
Of Him who once was slain.

Saints rejoice and ye sinners fear,
And heathens coming from afar
To worship at the glorious Star,
The Star of Bethlehem.

O may all nations joyful sing
Hallelujahs to God and King;
With Israel His glory He'll share,
Give an Immortal crown.

The Blessed Spirit is now come
To rescue man from satan's power;
From evil make them ever free
In Immortality.

The first coming was for the soul by the atonement—a free gift of grace without works lest any man should boast; and he laid the plans for the second coming, to receive his Elect unto himself. John 14:3. Therefore he comes the second time without sin unto salvation. And the second coming therefore is for the body, for he is the head of the church and saviour of the body (Eph. 5:23), and the time is shortened for the Elect's sake or no flesh would be saved. Matt. 24:22. Therefore the promise is the redemption of the body. Rom. 8:23. To say nothing of the types and shadows of these better things to come, set forth in the old Scriptures by Moses and the prophets, let us behold the gospel in all of its beauty pertaining to this great subject, then you will better understand the law and the prophets, and see what is yet to be fulfilled concerning the time of the end of the old world of sin, and the new which must now come in and be made ready for his coming, for he comes to receive his bride, who must be like him when he brings the great change from mortal to immortality.

Now listen! He came to abolish death and to destroy him who had power of death which is the devil (Heb. 2:14), and to bring life and immortality to light through the gospel, thus showing this is yet to be fulfilled, because death is not yet abolished, and the devil is not yet destroyed. And remember it is written of Jesus: He only hath immortality; but as the promise is: This mortal shall put on immortality, it stands a proof that it is yet to be fulfilled in this second coming. But they must be gathered and made ready. Ezek. 34:13.

Spoken of to Grow Out of His Roots.

Seeing this is a plain proposition, we would ask, what was the gospel given for if it is not to be fulfilled by his Elect, whom he foreordained and did predestinate to be conformed to the image of his son (Rom. 8:29), who only hath immortality? And as there was a manifestation of one son the first-born among many brethren, so there must be a manifestation of the second, and the sons of God,

Front page of the February, 1995, issue of the New Shiloh Messenger, an 8 page monthly publication since 1930. Benjamin and Mary first printed the Shiloh Messenger of Wisdom in 1903, on a monthly basis, sending the newspaper style publication to world-wide subscribers. In 1933 the subscriptions were over 1000 a month for The New Shiloh Messenger, on Mary's new press.

"Little Mary" Kolesar came with father and older brother from Glassmere, Pennsylvania, in October, 1935. In 1938, Mary Purnell would ask her to go into the Print shop and help out with the printing on the linotype machine. Through illness she was forced to retire from the linotype at the Printshop 57 years later in October, 1995; her 60th year in the colony. In 1941, at age 19, she was put in charge of the printing operation; she would print Mary's Book of Heaven, 1939; Book of Paradise, 1944; complete the 4th edition of the Star of Bethlehem; and print 680 monthly issues of the New Shiloh Messenger until her retirement as co-editor.

Mary Kolesar at her linotype machine in the mid 1990's. 680 months of printing the monthly paper on time. We have received many notes of thankfulness and appreciation from all over the world for her faithful and professional work in the Printshop for 57 years.

Hanon A. Smith, from Byars, Oklahoma became the photographer for the City of David; most of the photographic record from 1935 was the work of Hanon, which made much of this volume possible. He would also have a portraiture studio and dark room in the Studio Building until his death in 1974.

A Hanon Smith portrait of Joanna (Young) Martin. She with her mother, Josie (Lewis) Young, would come to the City of David April, 1944. Joanna's father, Carl Young, would come to the colony after his service was completed with the United States Army in 1945.

Josie (Lewis) Young came as a child with her parents from Washington State in the early days of the House of David, and would be in the circle of the "Shiloh Girls" later made famous in the 1927 trial. Josie was percussion in the girls bands from 1906, and would return in 1927 to give testimony in behalf of Brother Benjamin. The family, siding with Mary in 1930, gave them a call to come home in 1944. Carl Young would work several jobs including the "Job Press" at the Printshop until his death in 1986.

Gilbert Watts arrived from New Zealand in July, 1936. While street preaching in the north island at Auckland during 1927, he was asked by several who had fallen away during the heat of public ridicule of Benjamin Purnell, "Will you continue to follow this faith, with the papers full of these stories?" To which he answered, "The faith is the only thing that has given me something to live for; yes, I am going to continue to preach."

Around 1934, while helping out in the Correspondence Office, Eunice Bond would look upon the day's mail, and one envelope in particular. The postage was international, the return was from the Far East, one of the Pacific islands; but the address was in large letters across the entire front of the envelop: MARY'S U.S.A.

Foreign correspondents were numerous, as there were many in the colony that were of noticeable accent, sometimes quite broken English, and of foreign birth.

Alvina Grimm, Theodore Baushke, Louie Reinhart, and Max Blume were German born; the 3 Bond sisters, Gilbert Watts, Harvey Mann, and Andrew Ferguson were from New Zealand; and Kolesar family, and Joseph Stahon were Hungarian,

Peter Post was born in Russia; Nels Hansen, and Daniel Askerlund were Norwegian: Peter Smits was born in Austria; Michael Meaney from New Foundland; Melina Charter, Quebec; Christov Krishart, and Dorothea Decker were from East Prussia; R. Holms from Estonia; Henry Costello, Italy; John Van Dalen, Holland; George Nelson Denmark, Axel Sydow, Sweden; Nancy Berger, Cuba; Lillian Cartwright, Walter Trotter, and Albert Higgs were all born in England; Bill Totten, Ireland; William Connan, Scotland; the Vieritz family, Taylor family, Manthey and Anderson families all from Australia. These are a few names among the many that comprised almost 15% of the 396 signatures on the Roll Book of Mary's City of David.

1930 - 1939
The City of David in Its Building

Bethany (Left), Garage (center), and Laundry (right), all built in 1930-31.

MARY'S ISRAELITE HOUSE OF DAVID BENTON HARBOR · MICH. U.S.A.

Five log cabins starting with cabin #1 on the right were all built 1930-31.

"TOURISTS' CABINS - PARADISE PARK

East of the five log cabins, paradise park was begun in 1931.

Mary's SPRINGS - PARADISE PARK

SHILOH BUILDING

ROOMS RESTAURANT

PARADISE PARK

Mary's final head-
quarters at 1158
E. Britain Ave.
Finished before
Christmas, 1930.

Restaurant building
at 1204 E. Britain
Ave. Begun in
August of 1931 and
opened on July 3,
1932.

Mary's City of David appeared as it were, almost over night, as new parties joined in fellowship to the commonwealth of Israel. Shiloh excavation began on May 9, and seven months later Mary with her new home full would enjoy a Christmas dinner for 250 in the new headquarters. Other large building projects were also underway, such as Bethany (which was rooming, dining and the first floor Print Shop), the Garage (blacksmithing, auto maintenance, and rooming), and the Laundry Building (laundry, pressing, tailoring, and rooming), all of these buildings were of three floors, and completed by 1931.

The new beginning was the most exciting page in the now 200 years-plus-history (1792-1992). It brought people together in a working faith around Mary Purnell, as she at age 70, in 1932, would have her four books of the Comforter published, beginning with number four, and would begin to receive the 5th Comforter, The Book of Heaven, which would keep the PrintShop busy 7 days a week to keep up with the subscriptions, demand for the reprints of the standard texts, and the new forth-coming volumes.

The House of David Hotel Is Nearing Completion

The House of David hotel at Elm and Colfax Sts., which passed into the hands of Mary Purnell and her adherents in the recent division of the colony property, now is being opened up as a hotel after 10 years of idleness.

Alterations and remodeling have been going on quietly for months past, and the first floor now is practically ready to receive guests.

Started In 1921.

Started in 1921, construction was halted when legal troubles beset the late King Benjamin Purnell in 1923 and blocked the original intention to continue the building through on Elm to W. Main street.

For 10 years the upper floors of the building constructed of concrete especially patented by the colony, remained practically deserted, tenanted only by a few of the members, themselves.

Now the idea of a House of David hotel in the business district of the city originated by Mary and Benjamin, appears likely to be realized under the management of Mary Purnell, who is carrying on his work both temporal and spiritual.

The lobby of the hotel originally was planned for the portion north of the alley, and when this fell through, it left the present building without an outside entrance.

New Lobby Built.

One of the store suits on Elm street has been remodeled into a lobby. A stairway has been built and a shaft added where elevator service will be given in the near future.

Some of the furniture for the lobby already has arrived, and the desks and reading tables will be here soon.

The hotel has 100 guest room, 65 of which have private baths. The rooms are unusually large, each with two windows and a clothes closet.

When building operations were halted around 10 years ago, the rooms remained unfinished.

Now most of the rooms on the second floor are finished and redecorated. As soon as these have been finished, those on the third floor will be started.

All Fireproof.

The building is fireproof, being built entirely of steel and concrete. New lineoleum is being laid on the concrete floors in the rooms and corridors.

There are no dark rooms in the building. Every room is open to daylight with two windows, the inner rooms facing a large court in the center of the building.

The concrete fabricated both as to design and material under special patented processes, is noted for its gleam and sparkle and resistance to soil. The exterior today appears as fresh and clean as the day it was built.

The same material was used in the construction of the so-called Diamond House at the colony grounds off Britain avenue.

Approximately $250,000 went into the construction of the hotel, not including labor costs. It was built entirely of colony labor.

Property Goes to Mary.

Following the "split" between factions headed by Mary Purnell on one hand and Judge H. T. Dewhirst on the other, a property settlement was consumated a year ago last April which gave the building to Mrs. Purnell as trustee.

Her colony, which boasts a new administration building and many other new structures, now is flourishing on Britain avenue to the east of the original colony grounds under the name of the House of David as Re-organized by Mary Purnell.

Her group now operates a vegetarian restaurant, a clothing store and a bakery in the building. Plans are now being made for utilizing some of the first floor space to enlarge the restaurant.

THE NEWS PALLADIUM, Benton Harbor, Mich.
MONDAY, AUGUST 3, 1931

Mary's hotel crew of the 1930s; cooks, waitresses, janitors, bell hops, clerks and managers.

Left to right: Frank "Pop" Kolesar, Bob Griggs, Ed Reynolds, Alice Bond, Nellie (Bond) Young and Eunice Bond at the bakery shop on the first floor corner of Mary's Hotel

What the Bakery, and now the Hotel (by the end of 1932) gave Mary and her community, was an income source that was year round; unlike the Resort and farming that yielded from May through apples in October. To cover all the bases, there were many that worked a seven day schedule, at several locations, wearing numerous hats.

The "three war Bonds," as Francis Thorpe would dub Alice, Eunice, and Nellie, during W.W.2, were such examples, among many, of consistant and co-operative service throughout the colony, wherever and whenever needed; above their assigned and regular jobs.

MARY'S HOTEL

PHONE: WAlnut 6-7814   163 COLFAX AVE.

VEGETARIAN RESTAURANT   Benton Harbor, Mich.
One-Half Block South of Main St., on Colfax Ave.

One example of business advertising cards that Bob Griggs had printed on the "job" press at the City of David, which were distributed throughout the area, yielding a full 90 room hotel within weeks of the advertising campaign.

Norma Vieritz, Anna Kolesar, unidentified, Madeline Lambert, Bill Totten, Bob Griggs, Annie Griggs, unidentified, Joanna Young and Inez Buck.

Cooks, waitresses, along with managers Bill Totten, from Monaghan, Ireland, and Bob Griggs. Mary's Hotel would be operated by the City of David from August, 1931, until March, 1975, at which time, in a rare real estate deal, the hotel was exchanged for prime acreage along Lake Chapin, bordering a portion of the Rocky farm. Sister Annie Griggs would be Mary Purnell's favorite reader in the Shiloh membership meetings. She would cook, wait tables, can produce, and be along side her husband, Bob, for all 42 years in the hotel. Annie would also serve as a Pillar in the Church for over 30 years until her death in 1991.

Pictured above, center, is the Laundry Building, whose cornerstone was laid June 19, 1930 (under which was placed a copy of the New Shiloh Messenger, "The Little Book", and a Chicago newspaper), and the Garage (left) and Blacksmith shop. The architect of these three story buildings, along with Bethany, was Christov Krishart, from East Prussia, who also had been part of the team that drew up plans for some of the elaborate structures in the old House of David colony. Both Bethany and Shiloh would be occupied by Christmas, 1930, and the Laundry and Garage buildings would be in use by the end of the summer, 1931.

As stated above, a New Shiloh Messenger would be placed under the cornerstone of the laundry in June, and Mary had only vacated the House of David by April 1; so it would remain that printing was a priority. Mary was denied usage of the House of David presses, so her fourth Comforter would remain in typed manuscript form until 1930, when her new press would print and publish it first.

There were individuals and families, like the Griggs family in Oklahoma, and the Taylor family in Sydney, Australia, that during the mid to latter 1920's, would have their mail intercepted by the Dewhirst office in Benton Harbor. And these were virtually cut off from correspondence with Sister Mary for a time; Mary not having received her mail from them, and thus communication lines were down. By early 1930, lifelines were again being reestablished, and these families at last were able to correspond with Sister Mary, and finally to find out what had taken place there in the House of David.

In 1953, Andrew Ferguson would depart from New Zealand for the City of David, and before leaving he would visit a Brother William Wood, who had been in contact with the Sydney colony for a number of years. William had no knowledge of Mary Purnell, had not been aware that there had been a division in the House of David, and had never heard of the City of David. The Brother would write to Sydney with inquiries on the separation and Mary Purnell, to which he was never to get an answer.

PEACE

The crux of the separation centered around Mary Purnell, and her right to the leadership of the colony, after the death of her husband; and 217 saw her as the spiritual leader, to whom they would also go for temporal direction. The blessings of the Visitation, which began with Joanna Southcott's oral communications, would resume in Mary's new home. Beginning about 1936, Sister Mary would enlist Sister Jennie Martin to accompany her in her times of receiving communications, to write it down, long hand, as fast as it was given forth. What Jennie took down in haste, Sister Eunice Bond would put into proper grammarical punctuation; then handed on to Brother Arnold Nell to type; and by November 13, 1939, (Mary's 75th birthday), "Little Mary" Kolesar would have the 5th Comforter, The Book of Heaven, printed and bound.

Printed on a high quality, expensive, gold paper, "Inspiration" was a New Year's greeting poster given to the membership, and sent out to subscribers to the monthly paper in 1933. Included is a piece from Sermon 2 of James Jezreel's Extracts From the Flying Roll, and is the body of the written message.

City Of David Harvests Big Ice Crop

BENTON HARBOR, MICH., SATURDAY, JANUARY 23, 1943

**Left to right:
Jesse Honicutt,
Willis Baxter,
Otela Baxter,
Uber Tucker**

"As I am in this picture, it really brings back memories. Our family came to the colony in late fall of 1942. It was my first winter in Michigan. I had never seen such deep snow, and working on the ice pond was an enjoyable experience I shall never forget.

"I remember after each snow, a group of our members would go to the ice pond and push the snow off the pond with wooden push blades so it would be smooth and clear until it was frozen to the right thickness. Then we would mark the ice off into squares and use a gas buss saw to cut the sections. The saw was mounted on a sled and would be moved at a slow pace as it was cutting. The saw was gauged so it would not cut all the way through the ice so we would then cut the rest of the way through with a one handle across cut type saw. This was done one block at a time so the whole section of ice would not float out

in the water. When the blocks were cut, we would use long pike poles with hooks on them to flip the ice blocks out of the water on to the ice. We would then push the blocks across the uncut ice to a loading ramp. The loading ramp was very steep from the pond up to the truck bed. We would have to give the ice blocks an extra shove to get it up into the truck bed. It was very cold work, but I enjoyed it all.

"These ice blocks were hauled to the City of David Headquarters where they were stored outside, enclosed with rough sawed lumber from our saw mill. These ice blocks were a clear bluish color and we would pack saw dust all around them. The ice blocks would "keep" in this saw dust, even in the hottest weather. Remember everyone did not have a refrigerator in this era so the ice was delivered the following summer to our resort cabins to be used in their ice boxes, as well as for our own use."

Otela Baxter

1931. Background left is Bethany, to the right is the Garage and Laundry buildings. With almost 250 in number, a 90 room hotel, and resort cottages to supply linens to during the summer months, the laundry ran 7 days a week in the height of the tourist season. In the foreground is the Ice House location.

The Swamp farm, located where the Blue Creek joins the PawPaw River, was an Israelite farm purchased in 1905, and was awarded to Mary in the 1930 settlement. In 1930, the Re-Organization would purchase 75 acres just immediately westward of the Swamp, and the wet lands of the "Emmaus" farm would adjoin the Swamp. Each winter the colony would cut ice out of the PawPaw River, as in the above picture, and build an ice house to store it, which would supply the membership, the hotel, and summer resort until the following winter's ice harvest. In 1931 the harvest was 300 tons, by 1943 the average take was 1500 tons of ice, as the resort had grown from 30 rooms in 1932, to 150, and membership was near 300.

City of David Bakers at their Bakery-1930s--Leslie Reed, formerly a machinest at the House of David would become chief baker and specialty baked goods artist under the tutelage of Stephen Staubach. Left to right: Charlie Hermann, Everett Buck, Joe Shriner, Leslie Reed, Michael Meaney, Louis Buck.

Michael Meaney, from Top Sail, Conception Point, New Foundland, became a baker, and would learn the art of bookbinding, in which he hardcover bound numerous volumes of the New Shiloh Messenger, and other standard texts of the Visitation. He would also compile the invaluable Concordance to the Star of Bethlehem, type it and hand bind it. He would also serve the community as a Pillar for 10 years until his death in 1962.

March 15, 1930, just one day after the signing of the Roll in the big tent immediately north of the Bakery Building, the bakery ovens were installed and finished. The very next day Stephen Staubach would arrive from Chicago to teach a street car operator, a machinist, and several handymen the art of baking. Staubach was a former member of The House of David, and a professional baker, who was among those that left the Colony in the 1920s. Sister Mary would call on Steve to help her in setting up her own bakery in 1930. He would temporarily leave his Chicago employment, and stay for several months in creating one of the areas finest bakeries, which would supply the membership, a hotel cafe and bake goods outlet by August of 1931; and from July of 1932, a resort restaurant, along with the sales from the Bakery shop itself.

> *Oct 7th* ⚹ Kate Holliday, & the sick people at the 1st 80. Bakery still refuses bread. The children from 1st 80 went for bread to fix their school lunch. They were denied.
>
> Dewhirst sent word to old Bro. Reed thro Vernie that if he would come to his office he would see that he got bread. Bro Reed sent back word that that was like what satan said to Jesus. "Bow down and worship me & I will give you the whole world." but that Dewhirst need not think that he Bro. Reed was going to bow down and worship him, Dewhirst, for one loaf of bread.

As cited above, from Francis Thorpe's journal, October 7, 1929, the Dewhirst faction controlled the Bakery at the House of David. If you were standing with Mary, you didn't get bread. As the settlement day drew near, the bitterness grew to an ugly proportion, when Israelite children, whose parents sided with Mary, were denied bread for their school lunch. Also cited was the incident of Brother Reed, in his 90's, who would send back word to Mr. Dewhirst, that he was not going to bow down to him for a loaf of bread, as an answer to: if you stand with Dewhirst, you will get bread.

All the bakers stayed at the House of David with the Dewhirst group, which prompted the call to Stephen Staubach in Chicago, and providence of God kept with the ever faithful.

Harvey Russ would come up from the Jeffersonville, Indiana area to design and build the new Shiloh headquarters for Sister Mary, and then return to southern Indiana and continue a successful career as a builder-contractor.

The amazing progress of the first years of the City of David is due to the factors of how tight a working fellowship had developed in the years of enduring subtle provocations to open harassments, from the jealousies of exalted ambitions. There was a sense of unity, and a united front with a common goal at heart. It was a great release in freedom from the daily torment of rooming and co-mingling with the adverse faction. It was a pride in the determination of what is right, in the miracle only performed through the spirit of faith. And, it was just common sense necessary, for survival.

1902, Star of Bethlehem, page 141, 3rd edition, "The woman is at the right hand when she is in Jerusalem of the new world. Many in Israel will not drink this and submit; and through their lustful desires, the woman will be knocked down." Page 593 describes the Sheep separated to the right hand, while the goats would be on the lefthand. So it was by Divine Providence that Mary moved eastward, to the right hand, on any map with compass north.

Front cover of a menu from Mary's restaurant, the summer resort restaurant at 1204 E. Britain Avenue.

Mary's Vegetarian Restaurant opened its doors in July of 1932. There were rooms upstairs on the second floor, and the Resort Office was on the ground floor. The restaurant was in conjunction with the summer resort, serving a mostly Jewish clientele from May through Labor day until its closing year, 1962. The picture above was taken between the 1932 opening and the 1937 addition; they are from left to right: Albert Monier, Titus Smith, Max Blume, Ella Taylor, unidentified, Norma Vieritz, Daisy Edwards, Edith Dahlstrom, Estelle Hornbeck, Mabel Hornbeck, Margie Dahlstrom, Winnie Baushke, Gertie Smith, Ila Abbe, Goldie Honicutt, Virgil Smith.

The above picture, from about 1945; the Resort had grown to 174 rooms, and business was booming right through the years of the Second World War. The Vegetarian Restaurant was a great success because of the quality meals that were served from the fresh farm produce, and a vegetarian menu is a Kosher diet for the mostly Jewish resorters from the Chicago land area.

Pictured from left to right: Joanna Young, Jean Plaisted, Annie Smith, Gertie Smith, Bama Wellbrook, unidentified, Frances Honicutt, Melvin Tucker, Albert Monier, Mabel Hornbeck, Estelle Hornbeck, James Baxter, Frank Baxter, May Anderson, Goldie Hansen, Winnie Baushke.

Dinner 85c

Menu

SOUP

Vegetable Hash with Egg

Fresh Buttered Asparagus Tips

Glazed Carrots

Mashed Potatoes

and

Mushroom Gravy

SALAD

Combination with Mayonnaise

DESERT

Fruit Salad Sundæ

or Pie

CHOICE of DRINKS

Coffee - Tea - Milk - Buttermilk

Souvenir Menu from 1932 (Inner Cover).

The good old Restaurant crew of the 1940s. Left to right: Edward Greulich, Joby Couch, Homer Baker, Joyce Cartwright, Melvin Tucker, Mabel Hornbeck, Estelle Hornbeck. Seated are resort guests.

The home base of the 665 acre Rocky farm spread; it was the show piece of the City of David farms under the direction of Bob Vieritz. There were peaches, apples, plums, poultry, cattle, horses, grain land and timber on the farm, which was a precious possession for Mary in the 1930 settlement, and would remain productive through the mid 1960's. The entire farm property was sold, along with the Lake Chapin addition in 1991.

Standing L.-R. Melvin Tucker, Joby Couch, Malcolm Ayers, John Tucker, Peter Post; Seated, L.-R., Dick Callahan, Bob Vieritz, Uber Tucker, Julius Ayers. My favorite photograph of them all.

Bob Vieritz became, through the 1930s, 40s, and 50s, one of the south county's patriarchs of agriculture.

Rocky Farm packing shed

Apple time at the Rocky farm was an event itself. Using one of the Resort buses, a crew would be gathered up after breakfast at headquarters, and driven out for the day to pick and pack apples. Mary Vieritz would cook a spread at noontime that was worth the trip alone. The crew would return in the evening, and resume the next day until the apple crop was in. Among the many excellent cooks that prepared the homegrown produce for the Brothers and Sisters, Mabel Hornbeck, Monie Payne, and Mary Vieritz are usually the most spoken of. During the apple harvest, Mary Vieritz put on a Thanksgiving tableful every day.

1950 Haying time at the City of David
665 acre "Rocky" farm.

Timber on the Rocky farm would supply the Re-Organization with lumber in the early buildings of both residence and log cabin resort cottages. Produce, canned from 1929 at the farm, would serve to help feed the 217 in the first months of their new beginning; until fresh vegetable crops began coming in by the summer of 1930. Bob Vieritz also had a prize cattle stock, which he showed over the years, winning ribbons that would fill an entire wall of his residence on the farm. The Rocky was also a constant source of needed incomes with its several lines of produce; Rocky farm apples would sell all across mid-America to the east coast. Bob Vieritz was THE example of an executive; anything that was ever done on the farm, Bob had done all of his share too. "He would never ask you to do a thing that he himself had not done many times before you." Melvin Tucker. Like the many, many names within the covers of this brief volume, the name of Bob Vieritz was one that meant dependability, long hours, and immovable faith, as the Re-Organization was to prove.

KING DAVID HOSPITAL STAFF

Left to right:—Dr. Morey Lapin, Directing Physician and Surgeon; Cora Mooney; Dr. Max Thorek, of Chicago; Dr. Chas. Lapin, Chief Consultant, Chicago; Sister Mary Purnell, Trustee; Dr. A. R. Bloomenthal, Chicago; Dr. Joseph Silverstein, Directing Physician and Surgeon. Rear:—Dr. Raymond W. McNealy, of Cook County Hospital, and Professor at Northwestern University, Chicago, and Dr. M. J. Hubeny, Cook County Hospital, Chicago.

KING DAVID HOSPITAL AND CLINIC

Established at City of David, January 30, 1938.
The names and qualifications of the Members of the Staff of King David Hospital:

Dr. Chas. A. Lapin, chief of staff, is a specialist in endocrinology and eye, ear, nose and throat. He has been a practicing physician for twenty-five years. From 1923 to 1930 he conducted an eye, ear, nose and throat Hospital in Los Angeles, California. At the present time he is a member of many medical societies, and is head of the department of endocrinology at the American Hospital, Chicago.

Dr. Joseph Silverstein, A. B. and A. M., of the University of Alabama, and M. D. of Rush Medical College, Chicago, interned at the Cook County Hospital, Chicago, 1933 to 1937. He was resident in pathology at the same institution for six months. He is a member of the Berrien County Medical Society.

Dr. Morey Lapin, A. A. of University of California, A. B. of the University of Illinois, B. S. and M. D. from the College of Medicine of the University of Illinois. Interned at Cook County Hospital, Chicago, 1934 to 1936, and has been in active practice ever since. He is a member of the Berrien County Medical Society.

Among our consultants are:

Dr. Raymond W. McNealy, who is president of the Cook County Hospital staff, president of the Wesley Memorial Hospital staff, professor of surgery at Northwestern University, chief surgeon of Wesley Memorial Hospital, attending surgeon Cook County Hospital and Passavant Memorial Hospital.

Dr. Max Thorek, who is chief surgeon of the American Hospital, attending surgeon at the Cook County Hospital, author of many medical and surgical books. He is a vast contributor to medical and surgical literature, and is a member of many honorary societies.

Dr. Carl Cohen, who is a specialist in pediatrics, is a member of the teaching staff of the University of Illinois. He is a member of the Illinois Research Hospital, and is also a member of many medical and pediatrics societies.

Dr. M. J. Hubeny, who is the head of the Department of Radiology of the Cook County Hospital and a member of several radiological societies. He is also on the editorial staff of many radiological publications.

Dr. F. H. Falls, who is head of the Department of obstetrics and gynecology at the University of Illinois, the Illinois Research Hospital, and is chairman of the Department of Gynecology at Cook County Hospital. He is a vast contributor to medical literature, and is an attending gynecologist and obstetrician at several of the leading Hospitals.

Dr. J. B. Carter, who is on the teaching staff of the Rush Medical College, is an attending cardiologist at the Augustana Hospital. He is a contributor to medical literature and is an author of a book and several publications in cardiology.

Consultants, who are not shown in the picture: Dr. Horace Turner, Chicago; Dr. Leon Beiler, Dr. Phil Thorek; Dr. D. Spiesman; Dr. F. H. Falls; Dr. John R. Wolff; Dr. Louis Singer; Dr. J. B. Carter; Dr. Carl Cohen; Dr. Percy Goldberg; Dr. John Bellows; Dr. Fred Pollock; all of Chicago, Ill., prominent Physicians and Surgeons.

Dr. H. R. Krasnow, venerial and diseases of the skin; attending Dermatologist American and Willard Hospitals of Chicago; instructor in Dermatology, University of Illinois Medical College.

New City Of David Hospital Ready Soon

Dr. C. A. Lapin, Chicago, is chief consultant on the staff of the King David hospital. Dr. Morey Lapin and Dr. Joseph Silverstein, formerly of Cook county hospital, Chicago, are surgical and medical directors.

The King David hospital and clinic, which will have its official opening in about two weeks, is now assembling its staff of nurses and technicians. The hospital is situated off Britain avenue, about a half-mile beyond the City of David. The clinic is on Britain avenue, at Mary's City of David grounds.

The surgical and medical directors are Dr. Morey Lapin and Dr. Joseph Silverstein, formerly of the resident staff of the Cook county hospital, Chicago, and the chief consultant is Dr. C. A. Lapin, endocrinologist of Chicago. Mrs. B. Forbes, of California, is the nursing supervisor, and Mrs. E. Murphy, of Seattle, Washington, who has had several years of anaesthetic work, and recently completed post-graduate work in anaesthesia at the Cook county hospital, will be the chief anaesthetist.

Entirely Modern

The hospital is furnished with the most modern equipment available. The X-ray is a Picker machine that is completely shockproof, delivers 200 milliamperes, and possesses, among other advantages, a motor-driven table and a fluoroscopic screen that enables one to see the pathology as it is simultaneously photographed.

The department of surgery is very well equipped with the most modern type of instruments, including the Mayo-Balfour operating table and Castle Sterilizer. In the department of medicine, there is the latest type of Hindle electrocardiograph, a machine that is an indispensable aid in the diagnosis of heart disease, a basal metabolism unit and an oxygen tent with a motor component.

The obstetric department is designed and furnished to meet the various demands of the obstetrical patient, and includes in its equipment the most recent type of Hess incubator.

The hospital consultant staff is made up of emminent physicians and

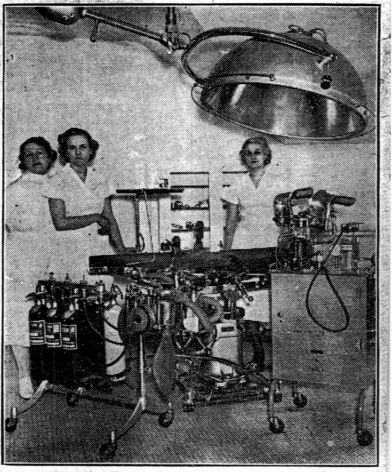

View of the complete operating room in the new King David hospital and clinic, established by Mary Purnell of the City of David. Mrs. B. Forbes, superintendent, is at the left.

Completely modern sterilization equipment is part of the hospital operating room.

surgeons of international reputation. The advisory board includes prominent local men, among them Supervisor James J. Jakway, J. J. Miller, Atty. H. S. Gray and T. L. Meyer of Chicago.

The Kosher determination will be in charge of several prominent Chicago rabbis.

The opening date for the hospital, with details of the program, will be announced in the near future.

The hospital project marks the fulfillment of a long-cherished ambition of Sister Mary Purnell. For years she has planned the enterprise and worked toward a definite goal.

January 15, 1938,
News Palladium

King David Hospital Draws Many Visitors

$50,000 Institution Will Be Formally Opened At Sunday Ceremony

Twin city and Berrien county people today were inspecting the new King David hospital, one of best equipped institutions in southwestern Michigan, which recently was completed by Mary's City of David near Britain road just east of Crystal avenue. The hospital can accommodate 35 patients and the outpatient quarters and clinic 35.

The latest in medical equipment representing a cost of more than $50,000 has been installed in the three-floor building. The directing physicians and surgeons, Drs. Morey Lapin and Joseph Silverstein, both of whom have been connected with the Cook County hospital in Chicago, have on the consultant staff many of the outstanding men of medicine and surgery in the middle west.

Formal Opening Sunday

The opening ceremonies will be held Sunday at 2:30 with Dr. Max Thorek as toastmaster. The speaker of the day will be Dr. Raymond W. McNealy, professor of surgery at Northwestern university, and president of the Cook County and Wesley hospital staffs.

The new building is located in the center of a 70-acre fruit orchard, and has been designed for the comfort of the patient and convenience of members of the staff. The institution is non-sectarian It is equipped with the latest proven devices in the medical world for general hospital work.

Included among staff members in addition to physicians are Mrs. Blanche Forbes, head nurse, formerly of Los Angeles; Miss Cornelia Sebeck formerly of Michael Reese and Mount Sinai hospitals in Chicago, laboratory technician; Miss Norma Loeb, formerly of Winnipeg General hospital and Mount Sinai hospital, X-ray technician; Miss Anderina Murphy, who trained in a Seattle, Wash., hospital and did post graduate work at Cook County hospital, anaesthetist; and Miss Eunice Bond, who is in charge of the office.

Has Modern Kitchen

The basement of the hospital contains a modern electrically equipped kitchen, special laundry for babies' garments with sterilizers, the laboratory technician's office, the X-ray room which contains the newest type of fluoroscope and X-ray table. Some of the equipment is of a type in use in Germany, but new to many of the hospitals in this country.

A special basal metabolism room has also been provided and it contains the newest type of electrocardiograph machine, the equal of which is not found this side of Chicago.

The hospital rooms have been laid out to give the maximum of light. The equipment is of the latest type, and the decorations and appointments give a colorful and cheerful atmosphere. There are two private rooms, two semi-private, four rooms of three beds, and two rooms of four beds.

The babies' room is reached from the second floor hall through a glassed in vestibule. A warming table, for changing infants and keeping clothing, is kept at 80 degrees temperature by means of electricity It also has an infant oxygen unit and incubator. A nursery is under construction besides the infants' room.

The operating room is on the third floor where an operating table of the Mayo-Balfour type is located. The anaesthetist has at her command a machine with which it is possible to give five gases. A three-stage operating lamp, and an emergency operating lamp which will furnish illumination for 10 hours in event of power failure, have been added. The latest type of ether vapor and vacuum machine for head and throat operations has been installed. It is of a type that is so insulated as to eliminate danger of spark from the motor.

The obstetrical room has a separating type table, resuscitating baths, receiving trays and other late features of equipment.

Notable among other features in the new institution is a special oxygen tent which is motor operated. There are special sterilizers including two bed pan sterilizers, a new thing in many institutions. There also is an elevator and fire escapes.

The outpatient quarters and clinic are three-quarters of a mile west of the hospital where remodeling and construction is in progress to accommodate more than the present 35.

January 29, 1938

At King David Hospital, April 30, 1938; from left to right: Blanche Forbes, Ruth Loeb, Ann Koshel, Norma Loeb, and Sister Eunice Bond. King David Hospital, on Crystal Avenue, between Empire and Britain, was designed and built by the City of David in 1937. For its brief history, the hospital would house the leading surgical equipment in America.

The Outpatient Clinic along Britain Avenue in April of 1938, from left to right: Dr. Charles Lapin, Dr. Morey Lapin, Dr. J. Silverstein, and Sister Gertie Smith of the City of David.

King David Hospital with its outpatient clinic was the most ambitious enterprise of the City of David, but would only last until August 9, 1939. Again it was big money with exalted desires that muddied the waters, pulling the two parties in different directions, and severed the contractual agreement between the City of David and the Jewish medical professionals and their financial co-operatives in Chicago. After several attempts for funding to reopen the hospital, the whole project would be abandoned; later the facility would burn and be destroyed. The present day Berrien County Humane Society building is situated just west of the hospital site, still surrounded by 54 acres of Israelite farming property.

1937 aerial photograph--headquarters, Shiloh lower left, King
David Hospital, left of centre, top.

Mary's City of David Resort would grow to 187 rooms, which kept a laundry, bakery, restaurant, housekeeping, and resort personnel busy 7 days a week throughout the summer season. The Resort brought good income to the colony, as well as helped to keep the tourist trade in southwestern Michigan booming.

Cabin #1, #3, and #4 were built and rented by the mid summer of 1931; Minnie Wulff was housekeeping. Frank Baushke was in charge of the first 5 log cabins that were completed and rented by the summer of 1932; and the City of David Resort as born, which would finally come to a close in 1976, with the last 2 Jewish families in #61 and #63.

Cabin #3 and #4 in 1932; the logs were cut from colony property at the Rocky farm and milled at the colony saw mill. The stones were laid and cut by Louie Manthey, while Melvin Tucker drove the truck bringing stone from the "Rocky" farm. Cabin #4 was removed in 1973.

**Sister Mary Purnell
with a family of
Jewish children at
her summer resort.**

Cabins #75 thru #79, 1936, Mary Purnell is right of center, wearing a broad ladies hat. The resort would need furnishings, which Francis Thorpe would buy from Newland Furniture in downtown Benton Harbor. The Newlands had given Mary a complete set of furniture for her empty Shiloh parlour at Christmas, 1930. Other furnishings were credited to the colony, and as business began to take the Re-Organization out of the red, Mary in turn would purchase resort furnishings from the Newland Furniture Company. Fundamental policy from the time of the Israelite beginnings in 1903: invest in your own community; buy from local businesses and suppliers.

"The Gateway of Prayer" Synagogue would be managed by Brother Baker in its 1938 building, and would be used by the Jewish resorters until 1976. An annex for the Rabbi's living quarters would be added in 1942, westward. The Synagogue would be seasonally used in conjunction with King David Hospital and the City of David Resort; the famous violinist, Israel Baker would frequent the resort with his family, and play for the congregations.

FROM THE GOLDEN BOOK OF THE JEWISH NATIONAL FUND

למזכרת נצח! מכתב תעודה
מספר הזהב שלקרן קימת לישראל

Provisional Certificate

INSCRIBED

№ A.T. 6-4629

In honor of
Sister Mary Purnell

PRESIDENT OF THE JEWISH NATIONAL FUND OF AMERICA

שם הנרשם

City of David
Benton Harbor Mich.

נשיא הקרן הקימת לישראל בארצות הברית

Chicago American

Dedicate Clinic Synagogue July 4

A large Chicago delegation, composed of leaders of Jewish organizations and rabbis will attend, on July 4, the dedication of an orthodox synagogue, built in Benton Harbor, Mich., for the convenience of Jewish patients and others on adjacent grounds to the recently erected King David Hospital and Clinic.

The delegation will be headed by David R. Balkin, chairman of funds and member of the hospital executive committee, and by Rabbi Dr. H. L. Goldstein, spiritual leader of the First Roumanian Congregation of Chicago. Dr. Charles A. Lapin, chief of the hospital's medical staff, and Rabbi Goldstein will be in charge of the dedication ceremonies.

Max Starr will be host to the Chicago delegation. 6-28-38

The City of David Resort was almost an exclusive Jewish Summer vacation home-away from home. The building of the synagogue in 1938, and the addition of the Rabbi's quarters in 1942, was a gesture of thankfulness to the Jewish community for their patronage that would last for over 30 years, into the mid-1960s. The tourist slump of the 1960s and 70s effected the resort business for the City of David and the area in general. And as Benjamin Purnell was quoted as saying, "Prosperity would abide, for the House of David and the area, during the presence of the messengers."

A few Jewish families would continue returning for a summer cottage until 1976 when they would turn over the Synagogue keys to the Trustees of the City of David.

6-28-38
Chicago American

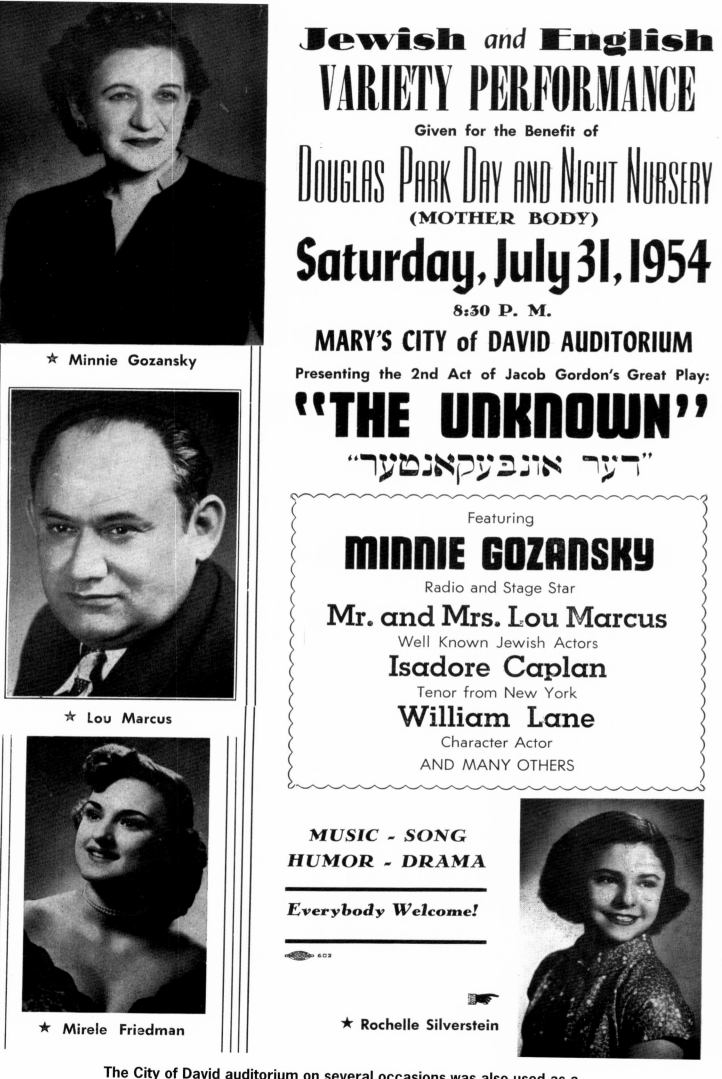

★ Minnie Gozansky

★ Lou Marcus

★ Mirele Friedman

Jewish *and* **English**
VARIETY PERFORMANCE
Given for the Benefit of
Douglas Park Day and Night Nursery
(MOTHER BODY)
Saturday, July 31, 1954
8:30 P. M.
MARY'S CITY of DAVID AUDITORIUM
Presenting the 2nd Act of Jacob Gordon's Great Play:
"THE UNKNOWN"
"דער אונבעקאנטער"

Featuring
MINNIE GOZANSKY
Radio and Stage Star
Mr. and Mrs. Lou Marcus
Well Known Jewish Actors
Isadore Caplan
Tenor from New York
William Lane
Character Actor
AND MANY OTHERS

MUSIC - SONG
HUMOR - DRAMA

Everybody Welcome!

602

★ Rochelle Silverstein

**The City of David auditorium on several occasions was also used as a
theatre for plays and speaking engagements.**

Public Meetings
Will Be Held By
Sister Mary
At Her
CITY OF DAVID AUDITORIUM
Every Sunday Afternoon
At 2:30

All are invited and Welcome.
NO COLLECTIONS

As Mary's Auditorium was being built from August, 1931 through the summer of 1932, the House of David Park Auditorium was being torn down. The Auditoriums in both cases were built for public sermons, and open-to-the-public meetings, from its beginning in the 1908 Eden Springs Park. H. T. Dewhirst had locked Mary out of the Park Auditorium in 1929, and would tear down the massive stoneblock structure in 1931; a structure that was once exhibited in Popular Mechanics Magazine. Dewhirst sited structural problems with the foundation of the building. But as it was, the foundation built in a half circle into the hillside could not be removed. So a fountain area was created, and a Beer Garden took the place of open-air meetings. While Mary would preach from her new City of David Auditorium, open to the public through the Summer months, from August, 1932, until the end of World War 2.

Mary Purnell, a bouquet of roses to the rightful heir. Her visitation would continue to blossom and flourish through the 1930s and 1940s.

PEACE

"Oh Beloved Ones,
We Love You
With A Love
That Exceeds All Else."
Mary

Baseball - Agriculture
Music
and the many hands of faith

The "Beehouse" above Eastman Springs was built by Harrison Honicutt; he would keep over 400 hives of honey bees for the City of David, providing honey and crucial pollination for the vast acreage of Israelite fruit farms.

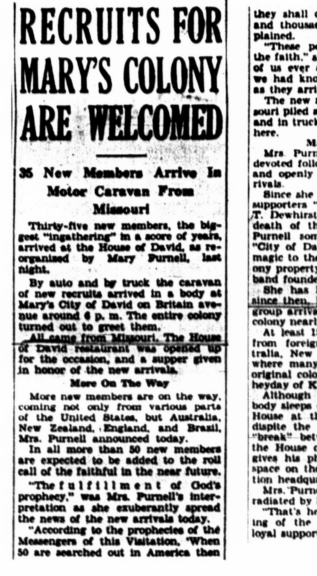

RECRUITS FOR MARY'S COLONY ARE WELCOMED

35 New Members Arrive In Motor Caravan From Missouri

Thirty-five new members, the biggest "ingathering" in a score of years, arrived at the House of David, as reorganized by Mary Purnell, last night.

By auto and by truck the caravan of new recruits arrived in a body at Mary's City of David on Britain avenue around 6 p. m. The entire colony turned out to greet them.

All came from Missouri. The House of David restaurant was opened up for the occasion, and a supper given in honor of the new arrivals.

More On The Way

More new members are on the way, coming not only from various parts of the United States, but Australia, New Zealand, England, and Brazil, Mrs. Purnell announced today.

In all more than 50 new members are expected to be added to the roll call of the faithful in the near future.

"The fulfillment of God's prophecy," was Mrs. Purnell's interpretation as she exuberantly spread the news of the new arrivals today.

"According to the prophecies of the Messengers of this Visitation, 'When 50 are searched out in America then they shall come by fifties, hundreds and thousands,'" Mrs. Purnell explained.

"These people long have been in the faith," she added. "Although none of us ever saw them before, we felt we had known them always as soon as they arrived."

The new members gathered in Missouri piled all their belongings in cars and in trucks for the long journey here.

Mary Is Delighted

Mrs. Purnell, "Sister Mary" to her devoted following, was visibly excited, and openly delighted with the arrivals.

Since she and her group of staunch supporters "split" with the Judge H. T. Dewhirst faction following the death of the late "King" Benjamin Purnell some seven years ago, her "City of David" has risen almost by magic to the east of the original colony property which she and her husband founded here in 1903.

She has had many new members since then, but this is the largest group arrival since the decline of the colony nearly 20 years ago.

At least 15 more are expected soon from foreign soil, particularly Australia, New Zealand, and England, where many of the members of the original colony were recruited in the heyday of King Ben.

Although King Ben's mummified body sleeps eternally at the Diamond House at the Dewhirst colony, and despite the admissions of a severe "break" between the co-founders of the House of David, Mrs. Purnell gives his photo the most prominent space on the wall in the administration headquarters.

Mrs. Purnell's spirit of enthusiasm is radiated by her followers.

"That's her real work—the gathering of the Children of Israel," one loyal supporter explained.

In 1935 the Payne and Honicutt families would unitedly come to the City of David in May. There were a number of trades represented in the combined family of 35 that would take the colony to its high tide in numbers, and increase the activities and enterprises to its height. This group would be the largest to come to the City of David to date.

I was thirteen years old when my family was called to the City of David. We came to Michigan in the spring of 1935--the call said, The Honicutts and all their families; there were thirty-five of us.

Preachers had been sent out to different states to tell the people about our faith.

I will never forget the evening we arrived at the City of David, Sister Mary greeted us so sweetly; we felt at home immediately. The Colony had all walks of life there: farmers, electricians, carpenters, plumbers, etc. We all fit in very nicely.

You will remember, there was a depression at that time; there was no work for the people, and very little money.

After we got the call, we all put our belongings, all we could, at an auction, to get the money to come to the colony in Michigan. We had three trucks and two cars. On the way up here there were very few places to rent, like motels and hotels; (we were coming from Tulsa, Oklahoma, and Springfield, MO). So we stayed in an old abandoned house by the roadside. Some people had seen us pass through their town. They called ahead to the next

town and reported us to the authorities as a band of gypsies.

So the next morning the officers came and asked us, "Why are you here and where are you going?" My father and uncle told them we were on our way to the City of David in Benton Harbor, Michigan.

We had our own laundry, print shop, green house, dairy, cannery, a large restaurant, a big hotel called "Mary's Hotel" which the farmers supplied the vegetables for, also for our own use. We all worked at whatever we were suitable for.

My mother was a cook and dressed resort cottages; my father was the blacksmith and plumber; my uncle was an electrician, and bee man; my brother delivered blocks of ice to the cottage ice boxes and for our own use. He also worked in our laundry. My other uncle ran our saw mill. As for me I worked at the downtown bakery store. I was a waitress at our restaurant, also at our cafe, in our hotel building.

We have never regretted coming to the City of David. It has been my life and still is.

Fern Baxter

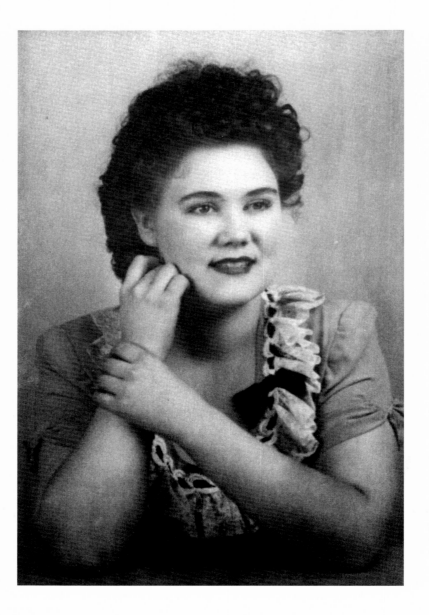

Nathen Honicutt

Jack Hurd

Malisa Honicutt

Francine Honicutt

Jesse Honicutt

Goldie Honicutt

Harrison Honicutt

Jessie Honicutt

Noah Honicutt

Merl Honicutt

Ralph Honicutt

Otho Honicutt

Morine Honicutt

Forest Honicutt

Maxine Honicutt

Slyvia Honicutt

Mary Lou Honicutt

Eva Honicutt

Fern Payne

Lois Honicutt

Jack Payne

Maggie Honicutt

Donna Jean Payne

Dude Ewards

Charles (Pete) Payne

Edna Edwards

Ruth Honicutt

Daisy Edwards

Virgie, (Hurd) Honicutt

Carl Payne

Ressie Norma Honicutt

Mona Payne

Ragie Honicutt

Cula Payne

Bill Payne

Young Israelite ladies at the Rocky Farm; L. - R. Fern Payne, Maxine Honicutt, Jessie Honicutt, Lily Dahlstrom, Marie Greulich.

"Pepper Game"--
City of David
Baseball Club.

L--R. George
Anderson, John
Tucker and "Doc"
Talley were the
stars of the "Pepper
Game", and
brought it to its
fame.

One of the 1940s
team--kneeling is
John Tucker, left,
Brother Melvin
Tucker (manager),
and George
Anderson. Doc
Talley is standing
second from the
end, right. All of the
other players were
hired players.

1934 advertisement poster which states the Club records for 1931, 1932 and 1933--impressive.

HOUSE OF DAVID BASEBALL CLUB   SEASON L(1925
1925

SEASON BEGUN JUNE 11th; and ENDED OCTOBER 18th., 1925.

NAMES	GAMES	AT BAT	HITS	RUNS	2bag HITS	3bag HITS	HOME RUNS	STOLEN BASES	WALK	SAC-FICE	K#	TOTAL BASES	%per cent
HECKMANN	98	343	130	51	33	8	7	3	30	9	27	200	379
J.Sharrock	56	216	77	45	12	8	10	11	20	4	36	135	356
WENZ	56	212	70	36	19	6	6	5	26	10	32	108	330
TALLY	78	323	98	59	11	2	2	11	6	15	30	119	303
CHAMPION	44	162	49	29	8	0	0	5	15	3	21	57	302
FAUST	121	510	147	84	26	6	3	18	39	13	77	194	288
TUCKER	89	315	88	36	14	0	0	9	15	12	68	102	279
HIPPE	88	337	93	51	20	4	0	12	19	24	31	121	276
HARRISON	108	391	107	53	29	5	0	15	39	14	47	146	273
BOOTHBY	75	272	62	29	11	5	0	10	29	16	55	83	264
WULFF	27	92	24	15	5	1	0	5	11	1	26	31	260
DAVIS	31	107	26	15	2	1	0	1	2	2	18	30	243
COY-KENDAL	96	329	79	47	21	2	10	7	33	10	112	134	240
PUP SMITH	33	103	23	8	4	0	0	2	6	2	37	27	222
L. MILLER	38	111	23	10	2	0	0	0	5	4	32	25	207
BOONE	54	165	28	16	4	0	1	1	8	4	61	35	160
EXTRA TRYOUTS	20	61	15	6	1	0	0	0	4	2	7	16	246
TEAM TOTALS	121	4049	1139	590	222	48	39	115	307	145	717	1563	281 272

average over 9 hits per game.
"   "   4 runs pergame K# means strike outs.

The young City of David home team of 1935; from the left, Louie Buck, Henry Tart, Melvin Tucker, Uber Tucker, Frank Kolesar, Cecil Tucker, Miles Crow, Ben Caudle, Everett Buck, Jimmy Crow, and Amos Edmonds.

2000 FANS WATCH FIRST NIGHT GAME

Under the even, powerful rays of 100 flood lights, the House of David defeated the Olympia Senators in the capital city's first night baseball game Monday evening, 4 to 0. Two thousand paying customers, the second largest baseball crowd in Olympia's history, saw the contest. The two clubs play again this evening, called for 8:30 o'clock.

Sparkling fielding plays by Jess Brooks and Loris Baker and the great hitting of Ira Flagstead featured the initial nocturnal affair. Flagstead got three singles in four trips.

Three Olympia pitchers shared mound duties and held the Benton Harbor whiskerinos to one earned run. The Davids got two unearned tallies the initial frame and scored their fourth run in the last inning on a wild pitch, without getting a hit in the frame.

Manager John Tucker delighted the huge crowd with his flossy fielding and antics at first base.

John Tucker was the most colorful of the Israelite stars on the diamond--athletically big league material and a showman both in the Pepper game and through the nine innings; he was a show all by himself.

The City of David baseball club toured with an equipment truck that could assemble poles, 100 flood lights with an electrical generator which brought baseball under the night lights in the 1930s, and a first for the Washington state, Olympia Senators. 2,000 paid to see "Jesus' Boys" bring "Enlightenment" to baseball in its most colourful days.

L - R, George Anderson, Miles Crow, John Tucker, Clay Williams, "Doc" Talley, and Lionel Averett brought the "Pepper Game" to center court, and the Harlem Globetrotters would pick it up and carry the basketball on to their own international fame.

George Anderson

Virgil Smith (center, standing) had the education of dentistry and medicine. He would take care of the colony dental needs, along with first aid attention. His fiery and infamous daughter, Etidorpha (Smith) Moore, would stay with the Dewhirst group, while Virgil and his second wife, Gertie would walk with Mary.

For a short period of time, at the beginning of the Reorganization, the City of David would own and operate the Gafill Oil Company, located on north Fair Avenue at Main Street in Benton Harbor. Pictured are Hanon Smith (left) and Ramon Nelson.

Mary Purnell, 1935

"Therefore the Tree of Life is known by sending forth such sweet solace which brings forth contentment, happiness and love, and is so strong and powerful that it penetrates so deep and touches the heart with its sweet influence." From Mary Purnell's 6th Comforter, The Book of Paradise, that she gave to the City of David in 1944.

So be of good cheer and write as often as you can O Godbe with till we meet again Yours for the establishment of Christ's Peaceable Kingdom here on earth

Mary

Mary would close all of her 291 letters with this or similar statement of joy and encouragement to her loved ones abroad.

Hanon Smith took this photograph of the banquet group in October of 1939, outside of the resort restaurant at Britain and Eastman Avenues. Sister Mary would call everyone in to the resort restaurant, after the summer season was over and the harvest was in, for all of the Brothers and Sisters to have an annual get together. The banquets ran from 1937 through the late 1940's.

Mary Purnell would write 291 monthly letters, beginning in 1925 and running through and into 1953; sending them out to correspondents, and interested parties throughout America and abroad.

During the year 1947, she would begin nightly meetings, that would continue successively for 700 nights, referred to as the "700 Nights". These meetings often last-ed into the early hours of the morning within her Shiloh meeting parlour. For those in attendance, her teaching and exhortation would leave a lasting memory of the inspiration and power of Mary Purnell, who in 1950, would turn 88. With the publication of her Book of Paradise, 1944, would complete the forty-two designated years, prophetically, for the Seventh Messenger to "sound". From the publication of the Star of Bethlehem in May, 1902, through the Book of Paradise, 1944, is the very fulfilment. Both in its content, and its completion of the forty-two years, in prophecy, The Book of Paradise, was given orally through Mary Purnell, to the confirmation of the City of David's membership in their choice of 1930, between Mary or the Honorable H. T. Dewhirst.

In 1945 the City of David bought the remainder of the Eastman Springs Estate, being 55 acres; with its famous mineral water springs that fed the wooded ravine from Empire Avenue to the House of David property of Eden Springs.

"Silver Queen" was the name given to one of the dozen or more springs in that immediate area. The water was once bottled and sold in Chicago, advertising its mineral content and medicinal value, which are on the sign over the spring, in the picture above. The Eastman Resort had been a popular destination for vacationers from the 1890s, with a number of cottages, and two larger houses for hotel rooming and banqueting reservations. With the purchase of Eastman Springs, in 1945, and Mary's farm in 1943, north of the Britain Avenue headquarters, the City of David property was continuous from Empire Avenue to Highland Avenue.

The smaller of the two buildings at the Eastman property was added on to in 1945 by Homer Baker, and would serve as an apartment building until its close in 1977.

Photograph from a 1907 visit to the Eastman Springs Estate by the House of David folks. Eastman Springs immediately east of, and bordering, the House of David property, undoubtedly was an inspiration for the Eden Springs park begun in 1907 and opened in 1908. Eden Springs was a 30-acre purchase from the Eastman estate by the House of David in the summer of 1907. There were 12 natural fountain springs that watered Eden.

The 78 3/4 acre Emmaus Farm at the north end of Crystal Avenue was purchased in 1930. The building to the right was on the property. The building center-left was built by the City of David. Otis and Winnie Baushke managed the farm which was later sold in 1993 to the Sarett Nature Center, along with the adjoining 91 1/2 acre Swamp Farm, totaling 170 acres, most of which is Paw Paw River wet lands. With extensive dikes, canal drainage ditches and a gasoline engine powered water wheel, the 2 farms were kept drained and would produce the finest quality produce of the numerous Israelite farms.

Harry Martin, in 1948, would take out an orchard, level the land (above) with his home made implement, and plant 15 acres of blueberries; which are in production and owned by the City of David today. When the "Friday Hoe" was first introduced for blueberry cultivation, Harry went up to Grand Junction to see the exhibition of the new equipment. He would return home and go to work building one, with its hydraulic arm action, for the City of David plantation's blueberry cultivation.

In 1936 the music "Studio building" was begun at 1328 E. Britain Avenue, and later in 1942, James Taylor would be in charge of the addition that would triple the original floor space, having 2 floors and a complete basement. The original portion was built for, and used as, a musical studio; lessons and recitals; voice and instrument. Later the colony would convert it into apartments with the 1942 addition; today it is a residence for City of David members. Hanon Smith, the colony photographer, would have his photographic studio, and darkroom in the basement of the Studio building, from which the City of David post card collection was created.

"Lizzie's Stand", immediately across Eastman Avenue from the resort restaurant. Elizabeth Truckmiller would run this quaint little concession stand during most of the 30 years of the resort restaurant. Souvenirs, pop, chips, baseball cards, chewing gum, and the like, were sold to the summer resorters at the City of David.

The City of David had dairy herds at the Rocky Farm (above), and at the Maryland and Swamp Farms also, which would supply dairy products for the membership, the resort restaurant, hotel cafe, and the surplus would be sold to local dairies.

Cutting sorghum cane on the 200 acre Maryland Farm at Berrien Springs. A five acre plot was grown, as pictured above in the harvest time of 1943, which would produce seven 55 gallon barrels of sorghum molasses, enough to supply the colony for an entire year. The harvesting crew would come as volunteers from all points in the colony to help Brother Harvey Mann get the cane to the mill.

ON MARYS FRUIT FARM.

The 70 acre farm was managed by General Robertson and his wife Ida. Today the farm is 54 acres with grainland and blueberries. Once the site of King David Hospital where the Berrien County Humane Society now stands. "The 70" acre farm was a 1905 purchase of the House of David, and its fruit packing shed would be rough accommodations in the Spring of 1930 for some who walked with Mary, until new homes could be built.

Peaches were grown on 3 farms; the 70 acre farm, Mary's farm, and the Rocky farm had a spread of 40 acres. Portions would be sold out of the 70 acre farm, located along Crystal Avenue, between Empire and Britain Avenues, and the peaches would be taken out. In 1948 a plantation of 15 acres of blueberries was begun on the farm, and with the remainder of 35 acres in grain crops; the farm is still productive today.

The Swamp Farm, on the muck flats, where the Blue Creek joins the Paw Paw River, grew the largest and tastiest strawberries in Berrien County. An Israelite purchase in 1905, and one of Benjamin Purnell's favorite farms, was awarded to Mary in the 1930 settlement. Silas Money would help oversee the Swamp Farm through the 1940's, and the farm would remain in agriculture through the late 1940s. The property since returned to the natural wetlands was sold to Sarett Nature center in 1993.

"Rocky Farm Apples"; pictured above is a 40 acre orchard of Baldwin apples, which were picked, packed, and at one time the colony drove their own produce loads to the distant markets of Boston.

Horse power was still in use on City of David farms through the end of the second World War; horses were raised on the Delvindale farm, near Niles, and on the Rocky farm, as in the above photograph.

Rocky Farm wheat harvest mid 1940s.

Horse drawn farm equipment at haying time.

Rocky farm at blossom time. Fruit in 40 acre spreads was a lovely sight to the eyes.

Rocky farm apple harvest. Uber Tucker would cut down an ash tree, have it milled at the saw mill, dry it, and make all the fruit picking ladders for the colony.

Brother Harvey Mann with his wife Dorothy, arrived in January, 1933, from the southern island of New Zealand. Harvey is pictured above with horse and wagon, moving sorghum cane to the mill for processing into molasses.

Swamp Farm bean picking crew were volunteers from the headquarters offices, laundry, restaurant, carpenters, and plumbers, that wore several hats, and made Israelite industries economical and abundant.

Dairy, grain land, and sorghum were on the Berrien Springs, Maryland farm along U.S. 31. Berrien Springs schools and the Berrien County Youth Fair grounds are now on the old Maryland Farm property.

Music will always be in the camps of Israel. Pictured above is a music ensemble from the mid 1930's on Shiloh's front steps. In Mary's City of David music would remain in the setting of social gatherings, and the musical accompaniment to the hymns and songs in the meetings, both public and private. Only Estelle Hornbeck, from the famous House of David travelling jazz band would walk with Mary in 1930; and from that time onward, the orthodox Mary Purnell would not sponsor or promote professional musical exhibition.

In the early 1930s there were several small music ensembles that created social get-togethers, and would provide an accompaniment to the services at the City of David. Pictured above is the string orchestra. First row seated on the ground are, Jimmie Taylor, Bill Martz, and Peter Smits. Back row is: Dave Faust, Arthur Abbe, Hiram Smith, Titus Smith, and Lawrence Abbott.

Emily Monier, Malvola Parnell and Fern Payne. "These were the happiest days of our lives." Emily (Monier) Gordon.

1946, Swamp Farm oats harvest under the management of George Baushke and Silas Mooney; the Swamp Farm also had a dairy herd of 35 milk cows during the second world war. Building to the left is the dairy barn, centre is the milk house and to the right is rooming with first floor dining room.

Picking crew at the Rocky Farm, Bob Vieritz on the ladder picking, no time for pictures. But then, Bob was in charge of getting the job done. In the early years of the Re-organization, the Colony would send Paul Perrenaud down into Indiana to purchase equipment from a canning factory that had gone out of business. Perrenaud would remove the canning equipment and bring it to the City of David and install and operate it to supply the Colony with canned goods and preserves in glass, or in #8 and #10 tins. The City of David grew it, harvested, and canned it for their use in a well-organized, efficient, and economical manner.

Berries planted in a young fruit orchard; getting twice the usage out of the land; straw berries in June, fruit in August, gave the land high productivity for sales on the fresh fruit market, and preserves for the Colony year around.

Hanon Smith's
portrait of
Inez (Grim) Buck

MARY'S BAKERY
CITY OF DAVID
Phone 9291

Date 29 - WHITE 194
M. 6 Lg - 33 M. Sup - 6

No.

29 # Bread Flour
11 oz Salt
4 ½ " Protane
7 " Short
1 # 6 " Cerelose
1 # 6 " Yeast (VAR.)

3 qts milk 3
5 qts water 5   8 qts

2 min Low - 5 M 1 M Second
Hobart

On September 2, 1948, Inez, at the age 16, her mother, Hazel, brother Eddie, and sister Stella would arrive from Ohio. In her first several years she would work in the Shiloh office with Alice Bond and then downtown in the bakery shop in Mary's Hotel with Nellie Bond. In 1953 she was called to the Bakery, then managed by Michael Meaney, and would remain as the sales person in the front of the Bakery until its closing in 1971. She and one of the chief bakers, Everett Buck would marry in 1967; and for those in the area who remember the heavenly aroma of Mary's Bakery and the delicious fresh breads, pies and rolls, Inez was the familiar face behind the counter for almost 20 years. Left, note sheet from Michael Meaney's recipe; 29 lbs. yields 6 large and 33 medium loaves; at the bottom is the shorthand notes for the Hobart mixer. Phone 9291 with your order.

On December 29, 1942, the Baxter family arrived at the City of David from Tennessee; in the family were the father, Willis, and mother, Margarette (pictured above), two sons, James and Otela, a daughter, Mirl, and two grand children, James Franklin, and Dorothy. At the time of the separation in the House of David, Charles Spriggs was staying with the Baxter family in Tennessee, who would be called to Benton Harbor to sign the register of names that were members who stood with Sister Mary. Having not enough money for fare to Benton Harbor, Willis and Margarette would sell their milk cow and his mitre box to pay the expenses for Spriggs to get home and sign in. In the dissolving of the House of David, each member was alotted a share of the colony value, which in turn was entrusted to Sister Mary, forming the Trust Fund that was the working money that began the Reorganization. So signatures meant money for Mary to start anew, and the Baxter family would sacrifice even necessities to help with the new beginning at Benton Harbor. With 8 children at home to feed, and Willis' profession as a carpenter, the milk cow and mitre box was an act of faith that God would provide in their struggle to survive the depression. The way home came by the end of 1942.

A group setting at the spring in Paradise Park between Bethany and the Studio building.

A group of Brothers in front of Mary's House in 1930, examining a fresh copy of the New Shiloh Messenger. A source of pride throughout its 66 years, the monthly paper would see two printers before Mary Kolesar, and seven editors in its continuing history, All of the written materials of Mary and Benjamin Purnell, as well as many of the volumes of the former six Messengers back to Joanna Southcott are housed in the City of David Library, since its commemoration of 200 years (1792-1992) in March of 1992. Reprints of the former six messengers are featured in the monthly paper.

Group photograph at the Emmaus farm, 1944, left to right, Joyce Cartwright, James Baxter, Malvola Baxter, Amelia Klum, Margarette Baxter, Dorothy Baxter, Mirl Baxter, Otela Baxter; on the tricycle, David Cartwright; seated in front, Joanna Young.

A group picture taken on the frontage of Shiloh headquarters in 1932. Through a determination of faith, and long hours of tenacious sweat, Mary's City of David came into being, and in 20 years would triple in size in its property holdings in Berrien County.

Later in the 1930's this photograph by Hanon Smith would be taken on the northeast lawn of Shiloh. Seated are, left, William Frye, and Francis Thorpe holding a "Shiloh" paper. Standing from left to right: Bill Bewley, Max Blume, Estelle Hornbeck, Michael Meaney, Albert Monier, Raymond York, Elisha Nelson, Julius Wilson, Fred Hoffman, unidentified.

Arthur Abbe was one of the carpenters of the 1930 New Beginning; shown above in this unmarked snapshot with one his helpers, perhaps an advisor. Arthur would later make, by hand, the thousands of building brick that would be the exterior to many of the City of David building.

A group of the carpenters in 1930's; pictured from left to right: Ward Lambert, George Nelson, Jimmie Taylor, and Bill Rein. Several of the earliest buildings of 1930-31 were built with second hand materials. A crew of carpenters and handy men would be sent to several demolition sites in the immediate area to tear down the structures for the lumber, and then bring it home to build with. The second floor staircase at Bethany is a visible example: the nosing on the tread show a hollow from many years of wear, but on the under side. Israelite carpenters had removed a staircase from another building and rebuilt the staircase to fit into the flight leading from the second to the third floor in Bethany; taking the worn tread and turning it upside down for a fresh and flat surface.

J. Andrew Ferguson was the last to come to the City of David during Mary Purnell's time. He arrived from New Zealand in March of 1953, and would see Mary Purnell only three times, one of which proved to be prophetic for him. While working on the new Resthome construction in 1953 with Albert Higgs, apparently against her wishes, he was called to the hotel with Bob Griggs to stand in for an ailing Bill Totten. He would remain with Bob until the hotel changed hands in March of 1975. Her wishes fulfilled. In October, 1975, Andrew would be elected a Pillar, and in May of 1978, would be appointed a Trustee, as the Secretary, until his sudden death in 1991.

Mary Purnell, pictured at 73 years in 1935. She would predict England's freedom from Nazi invasion, and in 1944, the New York papers carried her presentment of Hitler's death and the end of the war.

On the back steps of Shiloh are from the bottom upwards: Jane Ripper, Melina Charter, Nellie Bond, Eunice Bond, Alice Bond, Jennie Martin, Brother Weniger, Cora Mooney, Francis Thorpe, Mary Purnell, and Ethel Winterbottom. According to Eunice Bond this rather posed looking photograph was actually quite a coincidental picture, as all the above characters appeared within a few minutes of each other, and Hanon Smith was nearby, whose artistic eye saw this picture in the making. So we have this beautiful photograph, impromptu, from a summer morning on the back step; morning, because Nellie Bond's quaint arrangement of morning glories, covering the back step, are still in bloom.

A group picnic photograph from the Rocky Farm.

Left to right: Michael Meaney, Nells Hansen, unidentified, Tony Rubel

In her "700 Nights", and later meetings until the summer of her passing, 1953, Mary would exhort her people to stand faithful through the many trials in the perilous times ahead. She told those assembled that she would empty out building after building, until what was left she could put in her clothes closet.

The time would come that it would be unsafe to walk the streets of Benton Harbor by daylight; the jailhouses would be full to overflowing; there would be corruption throughout the land, from the White House, to the cop on his beat. Fresh drinking water would become a premium; and you would have to grow it, to know that it was safe to eat. Sexual promiscuity would prevail, and justice in judgment would be perverse. The planet would warm, and weather become unseasonable, out of season, and unpredictable, as the axis of the earth began to change. Social and political changes thought for the betterment, would continue the wars throughout the earth, amid the cry for freedom, equality, and peace among the nations of the world. There would come a time that people would pass by and say, "that is where the House of David used to be"; and "When the hope of Israel is gone in the eyes of the world, the Visitation would return in greater power than ever." Her admonishment was to always remember, where two or three are gathered together in His name, there He would be in our midst. "Men will think it strange to see women coming forward in these last days, taking the places of men in many walks of life, irresistible, efficient and worthy."

Among the multitudes in Israel that followed Jesus, he chose out from among them, 12. When Jesus would transfigure himself, he would take three, Peter, James, and John. Age or numbers has nothing to do with the power of God. It is the acknowledgement in the Truth of God, and your performance according to it through the trials of faith, that are the means by which one becomes established, as in faithful perseverance.

Emma Patterson, living at Mary's Hotel, would take a walk one afternoon, upon a notion, to visit her Aunt Bama (Mary's seamstress) out at the City of David. Upon arriving at Bama's door, she was surprised to see her Aunt standing at the door; Emma hadn't told anyone of her going out for a walk, nor yet her intended destination. She asked her aunt, "How did you know I was coming? Bama replied, Sister Mary told me you were walking out here to see me."

This volume would be entirely imcomplete without a small number of excerpts from a few instances, selected from the many voices of the witnesses confirmed in their faith in Mary as the spiritual Minister to her family of the Seventh Church.

Summer Resort: One of the Jewish ladies reported a diamond ring missing from her cottage. There was Quite a stir in the Resort Office--with no resolution that could satisfy the loss, or the growing anger of the complaint. Brother Baker sent for Sister Mary. She promptly came with Cora Mooney and several others, being filled in of the incident as she went. While crossing Eastman Avenue, she stopped, and looking around, pointed to a spot in the gravel road. There lay the diamond ring, to which Mary said, Return it to the lady from where she dropped it.

From Mary's Hotel, every Monday afternoon in the summer time, Bob Griggs would walk to headquarters to see Sister Mary. There were many occasions that he would take different routes through the lovely neighborhoods of Benton Harbor on his fresh air walks in meditation. Time after time, as he reached for the door knob to Sister Mary's room on the second floor of Shiloh, the door would open before he got his hand there; and she would proceed to tell him about his walk, and the streets he had chosen to come by. This time he had come by way of Eastman Springs for a drink of chilling spring water on a hot summer day; "It is good water, Brother, isn't it?" as she told him of his round through the Eastman Springs by way of Empire Avenue.

Francis Thorpe's office, on the first floor of Shiloh, found all three Bond sisters with Sister Mary one afternoon. As they conversed, Mary stopped and looked away in another direction for a noticeable time. She turned to address the sisters, asking them of their father, Hector Bond, who had died in New Zealand before they came over in 1933. Sister Mary began describing his features and stature to them, telling them of his presence with them in the room.

Upon Mary Purnell's death in August of 1953, Harding Dey was called to make arrangements for the body. Upon leaving through the throngs of journalists and newspaper reporters covering the Shiloh front steps, he would patiently ignor all inquiries, saving one outspoken interrogative in mockery. Mr. Dey stopped and turned, saying in a direct voice, "Be careful what you say about that lady." Upon which he parted the press of cameras and note pads in silence, as he departed onto Britain Avenue.

And the seventh angel sounded;
And there were great voices in Heaven,
Saying, the kingdoms of this world
are become the kingdoms of our
Lord, and of His Christ; and He
Shall reign for ever and ever.
Revelation of St. John 11:15.

And I heard a great voice out of heaven
saying, Behold, the tabernacle of God is
with men, and He will dwell with them,
And they shall be His people, and God
Himself shall be with them, and be their God.
And God shall wipe away all tears from
Their eyes; and there shall be no more death,
Neither sorrow, nor crying,
Neither shall there be any more pain:
For the former things are passed away.
Revelation of St. John 21:3,4.

Unto This Day

PEACE

SIXTY PROPOSITIONS

Philadelphian Church Whithersoever Dispersed as the Israel of God.

THIS ARTICLE, called the Sixty Propositions, was written A. D., 1699, about 300 years ago, by Jane Lead, of England, which is having its fulfillment today, in Israel of this Visitation.

1. There shall be a total and full redemption through Christ.

2. This is a hidden mystery, not to be understood without the revelation of the Holy Spirit.

3. The Holy Spirit is at hand to reveal the same to all holy seekers and loving inquirers.

4. The completion of such redemption is withheld and obstructed by the apocalyptic seals (7).

5. Wherefore as the Spirit of God shall open seal after seal, so shall the redemption come to be revealed both particularly and universally.

6. In this gradual opening of the mystery of redemption in Christ, doth consist the unsearchable wisdom of God, which may continually reveal new and fresh things to worthy seekers.

7. In order to which, the ark (of God's testimony in heaven shall be opened.) Before the end of the world (age) and the living (144,000) testimony which is herein contained be unsealed.

8. The presence of the divine ark will constitute the life of the Philadelphia church, and wherever that is, there must of necessity be the ark.

9. The unveiling of the living testimony within the ark of the Lord must begin the promulgation of the everlasting Gospel of the Kingdom.

10. The proclamation of this testimony of the Kingdom will be as by the sound of a trumpet to alarm all nations of the earth, especially all professors of christianity, because attended with the power of working all wonders.

11. There shall be an authorative decision given forth immediately from Christ to put an end to all controversies concerning the true church.

12. This decision will be the actual sealing of the members of this church with the name of God, giving them a commission to act by virtue of the same. This new name will distinguish them from the 7,000 names of Babylon.

13. The election and preparation of this church is after a secret and hidden manner, as David in his minority was elected and anointed by the prophet of God, yet was not admitted to the outward possession of the kingdom for a considerable time afterward.

14. Of the stem of Jesse, a virgin church which hath known nothing of man or of human constitution, is yet to be born.

15. And if it be yet to be born, it will require some considerable time before it gets out and arrives at the full and mature age.

16. The birth of this virgin church was visionally typified to John the revelator by the great wonder in heaven, bringing forth her firstborn that was caught up to the throne of God.

17. For as a virgin mother brought forth Jesus, the Christ, after the flesh, so likewise a virgin woman is designed by God to bring forth the firstborn after the Spirit, who shall be filled with the Holy Ghost and with power.

18. The virgin that is here designated must be as a pure spirit, so also of a clarified body, and all over impregnated with the Holy Ghost.

19. This church so brought and signed with the mark of the Divine name shall be adorned with miraculous gifts and powers beyond what has been.

20. Hereby all nations shall be brought into it so that it shall be the catholic church according to the genuine sense and utmost latitude of the word.

21. It must be an anointed church whereby it may bear the name of Christ or christian, being with Him anointed to the priestly prophetical and royal dignity.

22. Hence there will be no bonds or impositions but the holy unction among the new born spirits with all and in all,

23. This catholic and anointed church must be perfectly holy so that it may worthily bear the name of the Lord, our righteousness.

24. Until there be such a church made ready upon earth so holy, catholic, anointed, without spot or wrinkle or any such thing, so that it is adorned as a Bride to meet the Bridegroom, Christ will not personally descend to soleminize this marriage and present the same to His Father.

25. But when this bridal church shall be made ready and thoroughly cleansed and sanctified from every spot of defilement through the blood of Christ then He will no longer delay His coming.

26. There is not this day visible on all the earth any such holy catholic anointed church, all others being found light when weighed in the balance, therefore they are rejected by the Supreme Judge.

27. Which rejection and condemnation will for this end take out of them, a new and glorious church in whom there shall be no fault to be found.

28. Then shall the glory of God and the Lamb rest upon it, as the cloud upon the typical tabernacle, that it shall be called the tabernacle of wisdom.

29. Though this Philadelphia church is not known in visibility, yet it may be hid at the present in the womb of the morning.

30. Notwithstanding it will be brought forth into visibility out of the wilderness in a short time.

31. Then it will go on to multiply and propagate itself universally, not only as to the number of the firstborn (144,-000,) but also to the remnant of the seed (aliens), and strangers, against whom the dragon shall make war.

32. Therefore the spirit of David shall most eminently revive in this church, and more especially in some or other selected member of it, as the blossoming root is to precede the day of Solomon in the millennium. These will have might given them to overcome the dragon and his angels, even as David overcame Goliath and the Philistines.

33. This will be the standing up of Michael the great prince of Israel, and will be as the appearance of Moses against Pharaoh, in order that the chosen seed may be brought out from their hard servitude.

34. Egypt being a figure of this servile creation Babylon, under which each one of Abraham's seed groan, but a prophetical generation will the Most High raise up, who shall deliver His people by the mere force of spiritual arms.

35. For which there must be raised up certain head powers to bear the first offices, who are to be persons of great eminence and favor with the trinity, whose dread and fear shall fall upon all nations, visible and invisible, because of the mighty acting power of the Holy Ghost which shall rest upon them.

36. For Christ before His own distinct and personal appearance, will first appear and represent Himself in some chosen vessels, anointed to be leaders unto the rest, and to bring into the promised land the new creation state.

37. Thus Moses, Joshua and Aaron may be considered as types of some upon whom the same spirit may come, yet to rest in greater proportions, whereby they shall make a way for the ransomed of the Lord to return to Mt. Zion.

38. But none shall stand in any considerable office under God, but they who are tried stones, after the pattern of the chief corner stone, Christ Jesus.

39. This will be a thorny trial which very few (144,000) will be able to pass, or bear up in, wherefore the waiters for the visible breaking out of this church, are strictly charged to hold fast that which they have, and wait together in unity of pure love, praying in the Spirit according to the apostolic pattern, that they may be sent forth to multiply universally.

40. This trial must be of absolute necessity to every one in particular and to all in general for the constituting and cementing of the church of Philadelphia together, by the clearing away of all the remaining infirmities of nature, and burning up all the hay, stubble and dross which may have been added to the Word of the Lord.

41. For nothing must remain in this church but what can remain in the fire, Holy Ghost. For as a refiner will the Lord purify the sons and daughters of the living God, and purge them into perfect righteousness.

42. Through the operation of the Spirit in these waiters, they may for a long time contend with many infirmities and evils, yet if it be kept continually warm and watched it cannot at last but work out a perfect cure and bring a full and complete redemption from the earth.

43. There may be some at present living who may come to be thus fully and totally redeemed having another body put on them, i. e., after the priestly order.

44. This priestly, anointed body will render them impregnable, and qualify them for that high degree of spiritual government to which they are called.

45. Wherefore it requires on our part to suffer the spirit of burning to do upon us the refining work, fanning us with His fiery breath, searching every part within us until all be pure and clean, and we thereby arrive to His fixed body from which wonders are to flow out.

46. This body will be the sealing character of the Philadelphia church.

47. Upon this body will be the fixation of the Urim and Thummim, that are to be appropriated to the Melchisedecan order whose descent is not to be counted in the genealogy of that creation (under the fall), but is another genealogy which is from the restoration.

48. Hence these priests will have a deep inward search, and a divine insight into the secret things of the Deity, and will be able to prophesy on clear ground, not darkly and enigmatical, for they will know what is couched in the first originality of all being and the eternal arch type of nature, and will be capacitated to bring them forth according to the divine council and ordination.

49. The Lord, whose hand is lifted up, sweareth in truth and righteousness that from Abraham's loins, according to the spirit, there shall arise a holy priesthood.

50. Abraham and Sarah were a type of that which should be produced and manifested in the last age of the world.

51. The mighty spirit of Cyrus is appointed to lay the foundation of the true temple and to support it in its building.

52. These are such characteristics, or marks, whereby the pure virgin church, so founded, shall be certainly known and distinguished from all others, and whereby the action and true sound of the Holy Ghost shall be discerned from that which is false, base, counterfeit.

53. There must be a manifestation of the Spirit whereby to edify and raise up this church suitable to the ascension of Jesus Christ.

54. This manifestation must be the absoluteness of power and in the beauty of holiness, so bringing down heaven upon earth and representing here the new Jerusalem state.

55. In order to which, spirits that are thus purely begotten, conceived and born of God, can ascend to Jerusalem above, where their head in great majesty doth reign, and there receive such a mission whereby they shall be empowered to bring down to this world its transcendant glory.

56. None but those arisen in Christ in the regeneration (reformation) can thus ascend and receive of His glory; can descend again to communicate the same, being thereby His representatives upon the new earth and subordinate priests under Him, the Lord of lords, and King of kings.

57. Now He that ascended and glorified has made Himself our debtor, consequently He will not be wanting in qualifying and furnishing certain high principal instruments who shall be most humble and as little regarded as Daniel was, whom he will dignify with great knowledge and priestly sovereignty for the drawing together in one, the scattered little flock into one fold, coming out of all nations.

58. Therefore there should be a holy emulation and ambition stirred up among all true lovers of Jesus so that they may be the first fruits unto Him that is risen from the dead, and so be made principal agents for Him and with Him that they may be, if possible, members of the firstborn of Jerusalem above, our Mother.

59. All lovers of Jesus and true waiters for His Kingdom (in spirit) under whatsoever professions or forms that are dispersed, ought to be members among the Philadelphia Spirit to whom this Message pertains.

60. The society is not the church of Philadelphia, but consists of those who are associated to wait and hope in the unity of the Spirit for its appearance and manifestation, wherefore there is such a strict charge given them throughout this Message to be watchful and quicken up their pace.

Mary Purnell would publish and print only one of the many manuscripts of Jane Lead, the English prophetess of the late 17th Century, "Ascent to the Mount of Vision", 1699; and would advertise it on the publication listings from the City of David.

In her oral communications of the Book of Heaven, and Book of Paradise, there are passages that are quite exacting from this manuscript; as well as one particular article that is of length, and word-for-word, from a Benjamin Purnell article of 1916.

Spring 1990, a 1964 John Deere 1010 crawler purchased in 1989 and rebuilt with new paint by the City of David garage mechanic, Charles Payne; Author at the throttle, along with Charles Payne, operate our little miracle worker in its 1001 uses. Since the Spring of 1991, new renovation plans have yielded 9 houses with new siding, 28 houses painted, 25 new roofs, a new carpenter shop, and numerous interior restorations to the buildings of now 66 years.

August, 1991, Edward Grim left and Carl Payne, right, install new cedar shake siding on cabin #65. Edward's family came to the City of David in 1948; Carl's grandfather, Carl was part of the 1935 Payne and Honicutt Group.

Photograph from March, 1996; James Baxter, the Colony electrician for over 50 years, is in the basket of the City of David's latest equipment acquisition, a 1987 JLG man-lift. In the background are, left to right, R. James Taylor, Charles Payne and Carl Payne who are all part of the maintenance for the Colony: grounds, buildings, vehicles, equipment, and electrical. Building to the rear was built for the Colony in 1994 to house farm equipment and utility implements.

September, 1995; Carl Payne, carpenter and maintenance, oversaw auditorium roof repair in preparation for the new shingles in October with Kevin Peterson (right).

O Joyous resurrection glory,
  On this resurrection day;
Revealing God's eternal purpose:
  Life--for an everlasting day.
Christ in Jesus clearly showing,
  God's eternal nature--love;
In the mother's divine presence,
  That Jerusalem is above.
Joyous children of the morning,
  Death and sorrow passed away,
Crucified to lust and darkness,
  Willing to His word obey.
Peace on Earth good will to men,
  Again the angel's anthem song
Now on Earth in fleshen-bodies,
  The bride of Christ to him belong.
Children of the fallen Adam,
  Once again are given life;
And the children of the Latter,
  Being called the Lamb's bride-wife.
Once again this Earth a garden,
  Where the lion peaceful tread;
Once again God will gracious pardon,
  And restore us living-bread.
For all nations is forgiveness;
  The Lamb sent for a world of sin;
This is love's eternal nature.
  In the end, as it did begin.
Every mansion filled to measure,
  Every creature knowing God,
Every truth in divine pleasure,
  Coming from the chastening rod.
All His mansions rejoice together,
  The thirty, sixty and one hundred fold;
Reaping each as in their sowing
  And within His truth behold.

Easter, 1993
R. James Taylor

In everything give thanks; for this is the will of God in Christ Jesus concerning you. 1 Thess. 5:18.

As you are called, to be thankful,
　Showing forth the fruits of God;
Looking unto Him that giveth,
　Lessons from the chastening rod.

May we ever learn the precious,
　Understanding, hardships give;
May we ever learn the patience,
　And with humility to live.

With thanksgiving may we prosper,
　Quick to follow what is right;
In the midst of wrath's displeasure,
　Standing for the ensign's light.

Tears of joy from heart that's bleeding,
　Silent sorrows fill the eyes;
Long and lonely burdens heavy,
　Unjust weights that crown the wise.

May we be as faithful servants,
　Tried by storms--adversity;
May we ever seek his pleasure,
　Perfect trust, and steadfast be.

May we ever learn his secret,
　Crowned with thorns before the prize;
Love that can't be moved ever,
　In our hearts--before our eyes.

May we know His sore chastisement,
　Correcting in a parent's love;
Teach us truth in full measure,
　Before anointing of the Dove.

May we ever give thanksgiving,
　Amid betrayal of our own;
Abused--slighted and forsaken,
　Cutting deeply to the bone.

May you sing through persecution,
　Winging o'er oppression's deep;
May you always give thanksgiving,
　Sowing love for you to reap.
May God bless--and you to keep.

Thanksgiving, 1993
R. James Taylor

Shiloh flower garden with peonies and bird bath. June, 1989. Photograph: R. James Taylor.

Shiloh building, south exposure, July, 1995. Photograph: R. James Taylor.

The flower gardens around Shiloh were begun in 1931 and have been carried on through successive gardeners, among whom are the names of Joe Couch, Nellie Bond, and Joseph Stahon. In 1985 the author took on the joy and therapy of Shiloh Gardens. In maintaining and additions to the perennials there are now flowers from February snowdrops until November field chrysanthemums. Nellie Bond's arrangement of peonies is still the prize of the garden for around 30 years.

Shiloh Library completed March 12, 1992 in commemoration of the 200 year history and 7 Churches, back to Joanna Southcott, 1792. Photograph: R. James Taylor.

Christmas card from the City of David, 1990; along Britain Avenue at Spring Lane, looking eastward. The star of seven points is lit each year from Thanksgiving through New Year's day. The star was given a complete facelift and rewiring with new lighting in the fall of 1993 under the direction of the colony electrician, James Baxter, who has served the lighting for nearly 50 years. Photograph: R. James Taylor.

Elohim

O God, uplift us from, temptation's pressing dark,
  And gently guide us to Thy peaceful covenant ark;
Teach us earnest hands, and a willing heart
  Of Thy ever - Holy - Presence--never from it depart.
Fulfill our hearts with kindness, always for to know,
  That we become the reaping, of exactly what we sow.
To work within the light, of Thy everlasting day;
  To embody the Heavenly promise, become willing to obey.
O children of this kingdom, sowing faithfully, true light,
  Tender branches yielding fruit, Heaven's witness of the right.
Precious ones of Heaven's kingdom, by the Word conceived within,
  Purged from evil's ugly presence, so destroy the life of sin.
Carnal were these very children, before breaking of the day,
  The heart of God was so grieved, for His children once astray,
As darkness was to enter, to make manifest the light,
  So Lucifer was given, to prove everlasting right.
Those little ones enlightened, with the Spirit of Heaven's Son,
  By the Christ of God creating, two of flesh back into one.
As it was in beginning, so in the end it shall be,
  Man and woman are become, the Garden--fruit of life's Fair tree.
What was lost in Adam's sinning, is to be again restored,
  The righteous Eden of His pleasure, children living as Their Lord.
O God, be with us through, temptation's pressing dark,
  Keep us faithful-true, bearing crucifixion's mark.
For thy pleasure in creation, man and woman without sin,
  To re-create the peace of Eden, Christ on Earth is once again.

1991
R. James Taylor

They journeyed slow-she great with child
          Their taxes for to pay.
So coming unto Bethlehem,
          of David's descent were they.
The city of David--Bethlehem,
          Written in scripture prophesy:
The town foretold where Christ would come;
          So their journey had to be.
And finding proper lodging not,
          For young mother soon to be;
The Inn was full with hardened hearts,
          According to history.
The husband, Joseph, a carpenter,
          Had quickly to make-shift do;
The house of David they were of
          The Royal line it is true.
So young Mary's babe was born
          On a clear and silent night;
While wise men from the East,
          Came following the Heavenly light.
His star stood above the manger,
          Over Bethlehem a brilliant display;
These bearing gifts had distant come,
          Through Jerusalem on their way.
Come they all-who were called
          To such humble means as this;
To infant-king and Mother queen;
          Shepherds bowing, the Babe to kiss.
In manger-stall where cattle feed,
          She birthed him on the straw;
While Angelic host with songs of bliss--
          Perfect light the wisemen saw.
O glorious Light, Star of Bethlehem
          That guides us to Christ-Child;
Lead us to strength ever gently,
          so like Mary, both meek and mild.

Christmas, 1988
R. James Taylor

Auditorium build-
ing. Christmas card
from The City of
David, 1989.
Photograph: R.
James Taylor.

Bird bath at
Paradise Park,
Studio Building--
Christmas Card
sent from The City
of David, 1991.
Photograph:
R. James Taylor.

Mary's house as photographed in September 1995 upon a complete exterior renovation

It is given to me to see the approaching day in the spirit; therefore, if the representation be so glorious, what will the thing itself be when actually accomplished. Therefore this report, which the Holy Ghost has given of it, behooves all Israel to enter into the living faith, for it is the fulfillment of all those wonderful things concerning the reign of Christ, wherein must be terminated in the virgin seed, which will produce a new generation. Book of Paradise, 1944.

This is a state of life wholly peculiar to those that are born again of water and spirit. For it is not to be expected that others can live so untouched in the affairs of this mortal life, but those who are specially called out of the world to receive this Holy anointing, thus becoming priests, prophets, and messengers, to live and act in such a special way of consecrations, different from others that are not assigned to this Holy separation. Book of Paradise.

The bright flaming standard of Christ's personality will be of such magnificence as to draw home the dispersed and scattered flock, which have suffered greatly in this satanic kingdom; wherein a great Jubilee will be proclaimed by those to whom the dominion shall first come. Book of Paradise, Mary Purnell.

Mary Purnell in the "Marriage Feast" dialogue, written by Benjamin Purnell, and performed at the House of David between 1912 and 1914.

CAST THY BREAD.

1 CAST thy bread on the waters,
      Ye messengers of hope.
  And be thou not discouraged,
      For God himself will look,
  That every seed that's planted
      Shall bring, as 'tis said of old,
  Some thirty, and some sixty,
      And some an hundredfold.
  Far o'er the broad horizon,
      We lift our yearning gaze,
  And behold the fruitful increase,
      Return after many days.

2 Cast thy bread on the waters,
      However dark their breath.
  Nor think God's arm is shortened;
      He will save men from death.
  The words I give unto you
      Are spirit and are life;
  And his elect will ever,
      Be treasured in his sight.
  Over the golden threshold
      In God's appointed way,
  We'll reap the fruitful increase,
      Returned after many days.

Israelite House of
David, Red Song
Book, #89, "Cast
Thy Bread"

WE HAVE A LIFE MESSAGE FOR ISRAEL
WHO ARE SCATTERED IN ALL NATIONS

BELOVEDS: We exhort you by the mercies of God to earnestly contend for the faith that was once delivered unto the saints, which is the redemption of spirit, soul and body, which was the testimony of Jesus Christ. Therefore let us study to show ourselves approved unto God, a workman that needeth not to be ashamed, rightly dividing the Word of truth. Jude wrote to the saints concerning the common salvation, and he also exhorted them to earnestly contend for the faith that was once delivered unto them. Paul often spoke of both the common faith and the great faith. The common faith is simply the salvation of the soul, by and through faith, common to both Jew and Gentile; while the great faith is the redemption of the body without death, promised to Israel, who are now to receive it; and their mortal bodies will be kept alive, (Rom. 8:23,) and their mortal bodies will put on Immortality. The common faith is a way so plain, the wayfaring man, though a fool, may not err therein; but great is the mystery of the redemption of the body—God manifest in the flesh, which was sealed till the time of the end. Daniel 12. Broad is the way that leadeth to destruction—i. e., to the destruction of the body in the grave; but narrow is the way that leadeth to life, (i. e., the life of the body,) and a few there be that find it. The 144,000 will find it. Notwithstanding, many that went the broad way, having their bodies destroyed, will receive the resurrection of the soul. Remember, John saw them—a great company that no man could number, which come up in the first resurrection, washed in the blood of the Lamb.

Notice! The Elect, who find the way of life without death are a small number—not a company that no man could number, for they are numbered in Revelation, 7th and 14th chapters, 144,000, who are redeemed, spirit, soul and body from among men, and not from the grave like the great host. Remember there are different glories for man, as Paul speaks of the glories of the sun, moon and stars, etc. All receive their glory according to their faith and works. John says: Behold I come quickly, to give every man according as his works shall be. And Jesus said: When the Son of man shall come, He will render unto every man according to his works. Which will you have—the glory of the sun, Immortality without death, and receive an hundred-fold, or will you choose death, and get only the soul salvation, the glory of the moon, sixty-fold, a spiritual body made like unto the angels? for He is coming to receive His Bride; and those who are so found doing and keeping His sayings, will be His Immortal Bride—a body of flesh and bone—changed and fashioned like unto His glorious body. The blood will be taken away, and Christ, the Spirit, will take its place; then their bodies will be like His after He arose—sons of the Living God. Jesus said: If a man will keep My sayings, he shall never see death. And He said: Whosoever liveth and believeth in Me, shall never die. Believest thou this? Herein is the mystery: We shall not all sleep (die), but be changed in a moment, in the twinkling of an eye. But your bodies are to be prepared for this great change by the cleansing of the blood. Joel 3:21. He said: Ye will not come unto Me that ye might have life—the more abundant life, the life of the body, which is more than the life of the soul. Jesus offered them the bread of life, and they said: Our fathers did eat manna in the wilderness. But Jesus said: Your fathers did eat manna in the wilderness, and are dead, but I am that living bread that cometh down from heaven. If a man eat of this bread he shall live for ever—not as your fathers did eat manna and are dead; he that eateth of this bread shall live for ever. This bread is for the life of the body; for those referred to in the wilderness got the soul salvation, for it plainly says: They all drank of that spiritual Rock, (which Rock was Christ), and were all baptized unto Moses in the cloud and in the sea. Therefore this bread was for the life of the body, as Jesus' teachings and all the Scriptures plainly show. Jesus said: This is the bread which cometh down from heaven, that a man may eat thereof, and not die. John 6:50. Paul referred to those who ate manna in the wilderness, and said: Was it not those who had sinned that their carcasses (bodies) fell in the wilderness?—showing that it is sin that kills the body; and he said: The sting of death is sin.

Bodies that go to dust come up no more; and Samuel says: It is as water spilt upon the ground, which cannot be gathered up again. Paul rebuked them who believed in the resurrection of the body, and said: Thou fool, thou sowest not the body that shall be, but God giveth it another body—not the same body, but another body. It is sown (or laid down in the grave) a natural body, but raised a spiritual body—i. e., the soul. Therefore you see by these witnesses that all flesh that goes to the grave is lost, and the soul is raised a spiritual body. Not discerning the difference between the spirit and the soul, most people claim they are one and the same thing; but this is not according to the Word, for it is written: The Word of God is quick and powerful, sharper than any two-edged sword, piercing even to the dividing asunder of soul and spirit. See, it is divided; and Eccl. 12:7 tells us the spirit returns to God who gave it—which is one part; and the bodies of all who go to the grave return to dust, and as we have proved, come up no more—which is two parts of man; then what is it that is raised if it is not the soul? for Daniel says: Many that sleep in the dust—not the dust, but that which sleeps in the dust—shall awake. And Jesus says: Marvel not at this, for the hour is coming in which all that are in the graves (i. e., the souls) shall hear His Voice and come forth—they that have done good unto the resurrection of life, and they that have done evil unto the resurrection of damnation; as John the divine says: They live not again till a thousand years are expired, etc. What comes forth? Not the spirit, for it went to God, therefore it did not go to the grave; and it could not be the body, for it went to dust and comes up no more, as the proofs have just shown; therefore it remains plainly to be seen that it is the soul that is raised and reunited with the spirit in the resurrection, being made like unto the angels—not sons, for to which of His angels has He said: Thou art My Son? Angels are not called sons. But the earnest expectation of the creature waiteth for the manifestation of the sons of God, who are to have a body of flesh and bone made Immortal like unto His glorious body—the First-born among the many brethren of the sons of God (144,000), the Elect; and for their sake the time is shortened, or no flesh would be saved, for: This mortal (flesh) must put on Immortality. Jesus prayed that they be taken not out of the world, but kept from the evil; and Paul also prayed: May the God of peace sanctify you wholly, and that your whole spirit, soul and body be preserved (not destroyed in the grave, but preserved) blameless unto the coming of the Lord Jesus Christ.

GOD MADE NOT DEATH.

It is written: God made not death, but through envy of the devil death came into the world; and he that holdeth with him on that side shall surely find it. Satan is the author of death, but Jesus Christ came to abolish death, and to destroy him who had the power of death—that is, the devil. We hear people complaining against God—blaming Him for the disasters, storms and loss of life; but this is a great mistake, for we read in the Holy Writ that satan is prince and power of the air, and he is the author of all the destruction and death; for God willeth not the death of any man, but would that all come unto Him and live. Sickness and death came into the world by satan, and it is still so today. Jesus says: I come not to destroy men's lives, but to save them. And if you will notice, when Jesus was at sea with His disciples, there arose a great storm, and it was about to capsize the ship, and the disciples cried out: Lord, save us, or we perish! Jesus rebuked the winds, and there was a great calm. Now if the storm was of God, would Jesus rebuke His Father's works? Nay verily! But satan is prince and power of air, and it was simply satan and his works that Jesus was rebuking, for satan wanted to take the life of Jesus and His disciples. God is the "affirmative" and great life-giver to all things; but satan is the "negative" and destroying power.

It is His will to save flesh; and then, as it is written: They shall return to the days of their youth, and their flesh shall become fresher than that of a child's.

When we speak of the end, we do not believe, as many do, that this planet will be destroyed, but to the contrary; for it is written: One generation passeth away, and another cometh, but the earth abideth for ever. As it was in the days of Noah, so shall it be. Then the world was destroyed —not the planet, but the wicked people called the world. As it was then, so shall it be now. Then was the end of a world, or age, or dispensation; and then came in the Jewish world or dispensation, till they rejected Christ; then we had the end of another world, or age, or dispensation. Then came in the Gentile age, or dispensation, until the time of the Gentiles be fulfilled, and then should come the end—that is, the end of the third dispensation or Gentile age; as foretold by the prophets: I will overturn, and overturn, and overturn, till He comes whose right it is, and I will give it to Him. Two of these overturns we have already had—the first at the flood, the overturn of the wicked kingdoms; and the second, the overturn of the Jews when they rejected Christ; and the third overturn, which is at our doors, will be the overturn of the Gentiles, as it is written: The wicked kingdoms will I destroy. Then, as Daniel says: There will be a kingdom set up which will be an everlasting Kingdom, which shall not pass away. Now is the time that Jesus' sayings will have their full accomplishment—a time of trouble such as never was, nor ever shall be; which shall be war among all nations and peoples, till the wicked shall be entirely destroyed and the sons of God redeemed, spirit, soul and body; for as Jesus said: The meek shall inherit the earth. Then the whole earth shall be refined. Then shall she produce seven-fold, and the whole earth shall bloom in bliss for a thousand years, and nothing shall hurt nor destroy in all My Holy Mountain, saith the Lord; for Christ shall reign on the earth with His brethren, the redeemed— the people of the saints of the Most High; the 144,000, spoken of in the seventh and fourteenth chapters of Revelation, who are to be redeemed from among men. Then shall the saying be brought to pass: The knowledge of the Lord shall cover the earth, as the waters cover the sea.

THE PARADISAICAL LAW

The Law of the Spirit of life shall set you free from the law of sin and death. Rom. 8:2. After two days He will revive the hope of Israel; and in the third day He will raise us up, and we shall live in His sight. Hosea 6:2. The prophet here alludes to a dispensation—a day of two thousand years. After two days, or dispensations, Jesus came and revived the hope of Israel, which was the life of the body. Adam would not have lost his body had he not sinned—which was disobedience to the Word of God. God, however, has not forsaken His people, nor will He fail in His purposes. He has followed His people with the words of promise, and His covenants of life will not fail. Enoch, in the first dispensation, received the Immortal life of his body, by obedience, and saw not death. Noah, by obedience to God's Word escaped the deluge or destruction of the old world.

The Law of Life was given to Moses; and Paul said: The Law was ordained unto life. The hope of Israel was life without death—though they did not attain unto it because of sin, which was the transgression of the law; therefore their bodies fell. But Elijah kept the Law of life and did not die. The life of the body was the faith they held— i. e., the true seed from the beginning; but when the children of Israel were scattered among the Gentiles they lost the faith in part—saw the soul salvation still, but became blinded to the life of the body—therefore Paul said to the Gentiles, I would not have you ignorant of this mystery, lest ye should be wise in your own conceits, that blindness in part happened unto Israel until the fulness of the Gentiles be come in. Rom. 11:25. He saw at the fulness of the Gentiles, Israel would be gathered again (i. e., their descendants, the seed that was to come, to whom the promise was made, Gal. 3:19, viz., the promise of the life of the body. Remember, they had never lost the common faith. Their testimony was good, and some of them still held to the great faith of the life of the body.

Look at David. He said: Thou hast delivered my soul from death, wilt thou not deliver my feet from falling, that I may walk before God in the light of the living? They died in the faith, not having received the promise; therefore Paul says: There is something better for us—i. e., the life of the body is better than the common salvation of the soul. Jesus brought life and Immortality to light through the Gospel, and He never taught death. His teaching was the life of the body all the way through. He came not to destroy men's lives, but to save them. He kept the Law, as it was ordained unto life; and the Spirit of the Law of Life was in Christ Jesus. But they refused it at His hands, and He made the atonement for the soul; and now He comes to raise us up, and we shall live in His sight. He was a light to lighten the Gentiles for their soul salvation, till their fulness, and now He comes to be the glory of His people Israel. God has set His hand the second time to recover the remnant of His people, Israel, and His Laws come in force; as it is written: The nail that is fastened in the sure place shall be removed; (Isa. 22:25;)—which nailed the law till the Gentiles came in for the soul by faith. Now Israel will keep it as Jesus kept it, for He never at any time transgressed His Father's commandments. The 144,000 sing the song of

Moses and the Lamb (Law and Gospel)—not after a carnal commandment, like the Jews of old, but the righteousness of the Law of Life; for they are virgins, who are not defiled with women. Rev. 14:4. The kingdoms of lust must pass away and give place to the wisdom and power of God; and He that doeth the will of God abideth forever; (I John 2:17;) for they will overcome the world, the devil and the flesh—crucify the old man with its affections and lusts. To him that overcometh shall I grant to sit down with Me in My throne, as I also have overcome and am set down with My Father in His throne. To him that overcometh shall I grant to eat of the hidden manna which is hid in the midst of the Paradise of God, that ye may eat thereof and not die.

VIRGIN LAW OF CHRIST.

We Israelites do not under-rate the glorious atonement of Jesus Christ, for we know that the atonement saves the soul; and we furthermore know that to keep His holy Laws and commandments and all the sayings of Jesus Christ will save our body from death, as well as the soul. We are not under the law now. We would ask: Who is under the law, the man that keeps it, or the man that breaks it? The law was added because of the transgression, and is for transgressors; then the man that transgresses the law is the man under the law; and the man that keeps it in obedience is the free man of the city. If you break the law of your country are you not arrested and cast into prison under the law? But if you keep it, are you not free?

The great mystery of the Scriptures has been under seal till the time of the end. Daniel 12:4. Paul, when caught up to the third heaven, heard words not lawful to be uttered—that is, in that day, for they only saw as through a glass darkly; but the time was to come when a more perfect light was to be shown; for the vision was for an appointed time, and at the end it shall speak and not lie. Hab. 2: 2-3. Even the mystery of the seven thunders heard by John, he was not to write—that is, till the time of the end; which time we are now in. This Visitation of the Spirit of truth, which was to come, is given by the seven angels which were to sound in order. Therefore God's last message to man consists of seven parts of the great volume of truth, unfurled to the Israel of God during the time of the latter Visitation by the seven angels sent to the seven Messengers. And when the Seventh Angel begins to sound, the mystery shall be finished, as declared to His servants, the prophets.

PEACE

As stated in the dedication of this volume, it is only brief, for there are many more pictures, and so many more stories from the continuing history of City of David, unto this day.

As there is no such thing as unbiased account, there is either a leaning towards or away from a subject. However the perspective, there are the facts that will always go to the credit of Mary Purnell, and her community of Brothers and Sisters, known as the City of David. The credits should be recognized as saying, that none of the personalities behind the 396 signatures, over 66 years, have ever been imprisoned for a crime. The calibre of people that came from every point on the compass, from the ends of the earth, many of whom spent the majority of their adult lives in the colony, is a telling witness to the inspirational, and Christian character of one woman, around which all things of a community revolved. The array of talents was complete for the city they built, and maintain unto this day: stone-masons, bricklayers, plumbers, carpenters, electricians, cooks, mechanics, engineers, artists, musicians, nurses, printers, business managers, and farmers, as the list would go onto another page. There was a brief time, during the mid-1930's, that the City of David generated its own electrical power, had its own sewage treatment plant, and its own cannery for the preserving of the fresh farm products.

As Truth is the Mother Spirit, and her Children of Light, so this is a story from the record in progress, a story of many voices, long awaiting their time to be heard. It is a story in yet great expectation of the Millennial changes, long foretold back to Joanna Southcott, and the New and Old Testament texts; some of which are already before our eyes daily. Benjamin Purnell taught the people to stand by what is right and truth. For in the end, by reason of God, the truth shall prevail.

R. James Taylor
Secretary for the Trust,
Mary Purnell Trustee.
City of David
3-21-96

THE TIME IS HER THE WORD HAS COME
FOR TO GATHER HOME SAFLY GATHER HOME
AND OBTAIN THE GLORY OF THE SUN
AS THEY ONE BY ONE GATHER HOME.
THAT ARMY NOW EXCEEDING GRAIT AS
THEY GATHER HOME BRINGING EVERY STONE
FOR THIS GREAT CHANGE IN PATIENCE WATE
THAT BY THE SPIRIT THEY WERE SHOWN.
AND SPOTLESS THEN THERE LIVES WILL BE
WHEN THYER GATHERED HOME SAFLY
GATHERED HOME.
AND DWELL IN IMMORTALITY AS THEY ONE
BY ONE GATHER HOME

WE KNOW WE ARE NOT WORTHEY NOW
TO BE CALLED THY SUN UNTIL THE BATTLE
S WON, THAT S FOUGHT BY ALL THIS RACE
MUST RUN ERE THEY ONE BY ONE
GATHER HOME

IN EARTH AS IT WAS DONE IN
HEAVEN, THY KINGDOM COME THY
WILL BE DONE,
AND LIFE ETERNAL THOU HAST
GIVEN, TO ALL THAT COME THOUGH
THY DEAR SUN, TO THEE GREAT FATHER
NOW WE COME, AS WE GATHER HOME,
UNITING BONE TO BONE, AND GREET
CHRIST JESUS ON HIS THRONE
THAT THEY ALL SHALL BE GATHERED
HOME.

THE SERVANTS COME THE ROBE TO BRING,
AS HE NEARS HIS HOME NE)ER AGAIN TO
ROME, AND ON HIS FINGER PLACE THE
RING. AN ETERNAL TYPE UNTO HIM.
AND NOW THAT SHOUT WILL PEEL AGAIN
AS THE GATHER HOME BRINGING EVERY
STONE TWELVE TIMES TWELVE
THOUSAND WILL BE SEEN

LIKE TO HIS GLORIOUS BODY MADE.
THE CALF IS SLAIN THE FEAST S BEGUN
AS THEY GATHER HOME GOD S ETERNAL
HOME, BEFORE THEM NOW IS PLACED
THE WINE, THAT THEY ALL SHALL DRINK
EVER MORE.

TOU LIVING GOD WHO ART IN HEAVEN

From Hettie Purnell's school notebook, dated January 7, 1903.

Who is She
that Looketh forth as the Morning
Song of Solomon 6:10

Zeph. 3:14	O Jerusalem's daughter now sing
Psalm 110:3	Thy children with her rejoice;
	In the beauty of holiness bring--
	From the womb of the morning give voice.
Rev. 12:1	She comes for her people--deliver,
	Clothed with unwavering light;
II Corin. 11:13-15	A standard against the deceiver,
	Lucifer, the annointed and bright.
Zech. 9:9	The meek, the childlike, the holy
Psalm 50:2	Her beauty is the light of day;
	Like their master both humble and lowly.
	Israel desire to follow her way.
	This treasure so hidden away,
Matt. 13:44	Truth for the children of light;
	Their all is given to pay,
	For this secret of joy and delight.
Psalm 119:11	Thy word have I hid in my heart,
	So as not to sin against thee:
Rev. 7:12	Desiring to be as Thou art,
	For my heart ever thankful to be.
Ezek. 16:8	Thy covenant was given for love,
Song of Sol. 2	Commanding the knowledge to free;
John 8:32; 7:17	Sending truth on wings of a dove,
II Tim. 3:15	Anointing the child-like to be.
James 1:4	Let patience her work now perfect,
Rom. 5:3	Through long suffering is proven strong;
Gal. 5:22-23	Nine virtues of life to correct,
	Her spirit divides right from wrong.
Matt. 10:6	Thy kingdom come, my people rejoice,
Micah 4:8	Our princess of life is here;
1 John 4:18	The first dominion's daughter of choice
	In love that knows no fear.
Psalm 37:11	So meek above all in the earth,
Isaiah 66:7-13	The children, they flock after thee;
	Thy breasts hold the fulness of truth,
	Feeding the babes you labour to free.
Col. 3:14	Let charity's bond to perfection bring,
I Cor. 12:12	All our sisters--brothers, one;
Rev. 14:3	Let Israel's children the new song sing,
19:7	The marriage of the Lamb is come.

**Excerpt from *Poem for the Bride*
R. James Taylor, 1992**

Let us be glad and rejoice, and give honour to Him; for the marriage of the Lamb is come, and his wife hath made herself ready.

And to her was granted that she should be arrayed in fine linen, clean and white: for the fine linen is the righteousness of saints.

And he saith unto me, Write, Blessed are they which are called unto the marriage supper of the Lamb. And he saith unto me, These are the true sayings of God.

Revelation 19:7-9